D0599437

cookie Remix

AN INCREDIBLE COLLECTION OF TREATS INSPIRED BY

SODAS, CANDIES, ICE CREAMS, DONUTS AND MORE

Megan Porta

Founder of the blog Pip and Ebby

PAGE STREET
PUBLISHING CO.

PAGE STREET
PUBLISHING CO.

Copyright © 2018 Megan Porta

First published in 2018 by

Page Street Publishing Co.

27 Congress Street, Suite 105

Salem, MA 01970

www.pagestreetpublishing.com

All rights reserved. No part of this book may be reproduced or used, in any form or by any means, electronic or mechanical, without prior permission in writing from the publisher.

Distributed by Macmillan, sales in Canada by The Canadian Manda Group.

22 21 20 19 18   1 2 3 4 5

ISBN-13: 978-1-62414-519-3

ISBN-10: 1-62414-519-1

Library of Congress Control Number: 2017943527

Cover and book design by Page Street Publishing Co.

Photography by Megan Porta

Printed and bound in China

As a member of 1% for the Planet, Page Street Publishing protects our planet by donating to nonprofits like The Trustees, which focuses on local land conservation. Learn more at onepercentfortheplanet.org.

For my snuggly, sweet, inspiring, hilarious, cookie-loving boys, Elijah and Sammy.

Contents

Sweet Treats 115

Introduction

"Seize the moment. Remember all those women on the Titanic who waved off the dessert cart."

—Erma Bombeck

I'll begin with a confession. I am a cookie-loving, cookie-making, cookie-enabling cookie-pusher. I make cookies almost every day and I strongly encourage my children to consume said sugar-laden treats (I heard you gasp). Immediately upon walking in the door after school, each of my boys sees a cookie dangling in front of his face. "Try it!" I say. "But Mom, it's almost dinner." "Come onnnnn," I plead, except pleading is usually unnecessary.

My seven-year-old Sammy is particularly fond of sweets and every time he loves the taste of something, his sweets-meter goes off. If I get a loud "MMMmmmmm!" out of him, I know my cookie was a success. If the "MMMmmmmm!" sounds like a muffled, excited scream and lasts more than ten seconds, I know it was a crazy success. Most of the cookies in this book were crazy successes in Sammy's opinion, minus only the ones that sat on the top shelf of our fridge with the NO KIDS sign taped to them because they contained alcohol and/or caffeine. Now that I think of it, a more appropriate sign would have been FOR MOMMY.

In all honesty, cookies have not always been my thing. I mean, I have always loved eating cookies, but I have not always been a fanatical maker of cookies. A recurring theme in my life has been becoming deeply passionate about (obsessed with) one particular thing and turning it into the coolest, yummiest, prettiest, most fun, most amazing thing (to me) ever. Some of my past obsessions: hula-hooping, sunset oil paintings, falling really fast from the sky after jumping out of an airplane (217 mph personal record!), salad creations, yo-yo moves, haiku poems, grilled cheese sandwiches and food photography.

In the past few years, the good ol' cookie has popped up on my radar as a subject for creative expression. Its shining potential and endless possibilities have been unveiled. The word *cookie* is like a blank canvas staring me down, inviting me to pull out my paints and bucket of turpentine. There are so many exciting flavors, textures, toppings and colors to choose from! The only thing that excites me more than this never-ending string of possibilities is watching people's faces as they bite into of one of my creations.

Rarely do I have a brilliant idea during waking hours. Most of my really good ideas come to me in my sleep. One night not too long ago, my husband and I were enjoying a night away in a nearby hotel. We had stuffed our faces with sushi and drank our share of wine and fell quickly asleep with full, satisfied bellies, because that's what tired parents do when they have time alone. At some point early in my sleeping hours, I had the idea that I needed to create cookies inspired by already established delicious treats. Drinks, cakes, pies, ice cream, pancakes, cinnamon rolls, smoothies, sodas, donuts . . . the options were absolutely endless! I woke from dreams of cookies and donuts doing synchronized swimming together, and I was ready to start baking. That is how this deliciously irresistible collection of recipes was born.

Since that night, I have not stopped conjuring up marriages between cookies and sweets of varying kinds. Figuring out how to turn a creamy pie or an ice cream flavor into a 3-inch (4.5-cm) cookie has satisfied my deepest creative and sweets-loving desires. This has been my most satisfying obsession to date, which is saying a lot because skydiving is *really* fun.

Have you ever had a dessert pop into your thoughts, followed by a burning need to have it sitting in front of you? Then you remember that many desserts require tireless work to prepare? "As easy as pie" is the dumbest saying ever, in my opinion, because pie is not easy, people. Pies require ridiculous, painstaking effort. Cakes require multiple steps and tons of patience. Cinnamon rolls take forever to make, with all of the rising and resting and kneading. And to be honest, I can't often eat an entire slice of pie in a single sitting, so it seems like a waste to go out and buy one. Enjoying the flavors of my favorite sweet treats in a few bites and with minimal effort is a dream come true.

The cookies in this book are game changers. You will blow people away with these recipes. I know this because I personally swooned over every single cookie in this book. Every one of them made my heart sing and my shoes pop right off my feet. I received rave reviews about the cookies I shared with others, as well. Specific comments are littered throughout the pages that follow, but for further proof I'll let the words of my sweet but honest boys be the final say:

· ·

Hubby Dan: "Wife, your cookies are creative and absolutely delicious."

Elijah (age 10): "I think your cookies are so awesome, Mom. They all are so delicious that my head could possibly explode. I loved coming home after school to see what you had made every day."

Sammy (age 7): "All your cookies are so delicious. They are so good that I think my mind turned into a sugar cookie!"

· ·

Note: Be sure to check out my resources (pages 166 to 171) for more information on equipment, ovens, ingredients, quick fixes and storage!

Terminology

Two of the methods used for getting the batter, once mixed, onto the baking sheets are worthy of clarification before diving in.

Drop cookies describe batter that is generally a bit too gooey to handle, requiring a cookie scoop or spoon to drop it into position on the baking sheets. Once on the baking sheet, it should not be touched or moved unless otherwise specified in the recipe.

If a dough is firm enough to be handled, the instructions will note to measure it out with the appropriately-sized scoop or spoon, shape the dough with your hands or fingers and place it onto the baking sheet.

Go Make Cookies!

Read through each recipe in its entirety before preheating your oven. You'll want to make sure you have all the ingredients and that you fully understand every part of the instructions before you start. The scrumptious cookies in this book are waiting for you, so go on! Mix, bake, frost, enjoy and share!

But first, a cookie interview with my favorite cookie testers:

· ·

Me: If you could turn into any cookie in this book, what would it be and why?

Elijah (age 10): A Strawberry Sprinkle Donut Cookie, because I really want to be a donut.

Sammy (age 7): I'd turn into a Strawberry Sprinkle Donut Cookie, because strawberries are my favorite fruit.

Me: Do you think you'll make cookies when you grow up? If so, which kinds?

E: Yeah, maybe. I'll make your Key Lime Pie Cookies, if I do.

S: I think when I grow up I'll make a lot of cake-flavored cookies.

Me: What cookies is this book missing?

E: A Peanut Butter and Jelly Cookie! Also, you can't forget a Strawberry Banana Smoothie Cookie next time.

S: You should have made a Lemon Meringue Pie Cookie. Also a Milk Chocolate Bar Cookie.

Me: Is there anything you'd rather eat than my cookies?

E: Lollipops.

S: There's nothing that could be more delicious, Mom.

Me: Do you think Sammy can control his Mmmmmming when he enjoys a cookie?/Can you control your Mmmmmming when you enjoy a cookie?

E: He cannot control it.

S: No, I cannot.

Me: What was Daddy's favorite cookie?

E: The one with both alcohol and caffeine.

S: Maybe Chocolate Peanut?

Me: If I write another cookbook, what should it be about?

E: MORE cookies! It should be a Cookies and Toast cookbook!

S: You should write about all kinds of cakes!

Me: What is your favorite part about helping make cookies?

E: Mixing the batter.

S: Turning on the mixer.

Me: What questions do you have for me?

E: What was your favorite cookie, Mom? (Read on for the answer!)

S: Will you ever make more drink-flavored cookies? Because I have a lot more ideas for you. (Yes. Yes, I will.)

Drinks

Cookies inspired by soda, coffee and more!

My family's favorites from this section:

Me: Dark Roast Coffee Cookies (page 17)—The deep richness of this cookie combined with the gooey dark chocolate and extra caffeine kick made it my favorite of all of the drink-inspired cookies!

Hubby Dan: White Russian Cookies (page 21)—"I *had* to make a White Russian immediately after eating it because it was so good and tasted so much like the drink. It was the first cookie that broke down my willpower. I had no self-control and ate three in a row."

Elijah (age 10): Cherry Cola Cookies (page 22)—"It was amazing!"

Sammy (age 7): Cherry Lemon-Lime Cookies (page 14)—"I loved that cookie because I really like cherries."

Creating cookies inspired by drinks was the first idea that got me excited about this cookbook. There are so many different types of beverages to enjoy and they are enjoyed for endless reasons. Drinks can be thirst-quenching, relaxing, refreshing, stimulating and comforting. They can be rich, light, spicy, sweet, creamy, sparkly and fruity. Drinks are a staple at every type of meal or event, whether it's a simple dinner alone or a party with hundreds of people.

I have loved transforming my favorite beverages into cookies. What has been even more fun is watching a friend bite into a cookie followed by, "This tastes *just* like a can of Cherry Coke!" I have always loved adding surprise elements to food, whether it's a secret spice in mashed potatoes or a piece of candy hidden inside a brownie. Combining beverages with cookies has been fun and delicious!

Root Beer Float Cookies

There are a handful of perfect flavor combinations that were just meant to find one another, root beer and vanilla ice cream being one of them. Drinking a root beer float brings me back to hot summer days spent with my dad in Iowa. I created this cookie with so much love, thinking back on those wonderful, carefree days of childhood. It could not have tasted more true to the summer treat. I shared a few with a friend and the first word out of her mouth was, "childhood."

COOKIES

¾ cup (1½ sticks; 167 g) salted butter, softened

1 cup (225 g) light brown sugar

½ cup (100 g) granulated sugar

2 large eggs

2 tsp (10 ml) root beer concentrate, or 5 tbsp (45 ml) root beer

3 tbsp (45 ml) milk

3 cups (375 g) all-purpose flour

1½ tsp (7 g) baking soda

1 tsp (6 g) salt

FROSTING

½ cup (1 stick; 112 g) salted butter, softened

3 cups (360 g) confectioners' sugar

1 tsp (5 ml) root beer concentrate, or 2 to 3 tbsp (30 to 45 ml) root beer

1 to 3 tbsp (15 to 45 ml) milk

MAKE THE COOKIES

Preheat the oven to 350°F (180°C) and line 3 baking sheets with parchment paper. Using a stand mixer fitted with the paddle attachment (or a large mixing bowl with a hand mixer), combine the butter, brown and granulated sugar, eggs, root beer concentrate and milk and beat on medium speed until creamy and free of lumps.

In a separate bowl, combine the flour, baking soda and salt. Mix well. Gradually add to the butter mixture and beat on medium speed until just combined.

Using a medium cookie scoop, drop the dough by 1½ tablespoons (22.5 g) 2 inches (5 cm) apart onto the prepared baking sheets. Bake in the preheated oven for 9 to 11 minutes, or until golden brown around the bottom edges with no uncooked dough in the centers. Remove from the oven and transfer the cookies to a wire rack and let cool.

MAKE THE FROSTING

Using a stand mixer fitted with the whisk attachment (or a large mixing bowl with a hand mixer), combine the butter, confectioners' sugar and root beer concentrate. Add the milk 1 tablespoon (15 ml) at a time until the desired consistency is reached. Beat on medium speed for 3 minutes.

ASSEMBLE THE COOKIES

Spread the frosting over the cookies.

Cherry Lemon-Lime Cookies

MAKES 38 COOKIES

Whoever had the idea to combine cherries with lemons and limes is my hero. I am a huge fan of cherries with anything, but somehow this trio is extra exciting. I love Cherry 7UP for this reason and this cookie is the perfect replica of the refreshing drink!

COOKIES
¾ cup (1½ sticks; 167 g) salted butter, softened

1½ cups (300 g) granulated sugar, plus more for sprinkling

1 large egg

¼ cup (60 ml) cherry lemon-lime soda, such as Cherry 7UP

2½ cups (310 g) all-purpose flour

1½ tsp (7 g) baking powder

1 tsp (6 g) salt

2 tbsp (30 ml) liquid from maraschino cherry jar

Red food coloring

Zest of 1 lime (about 1 tbsp [9 g])

Zest of 1 lemon (about 1 tbsp [9 g])

Green food coloring

TOPPING
38 maraschino cherries

MAKE THE COOKIES
Preheat the oven to 350°F (180°C) and line 3 baking sheets with parchment paper. Using a stand mixer fitted with the paddle attachment (or a large mixing bowl with a hand mixer), combine the butter, granulated sugar, egg and soda and beat on medium speed until creamy and free of lumps.

In a separate bowl, combine the flour, baking powder and salt. Mix well. Gradually add to the butter mixture and beat on medium speed until just combined.

Transfer half of the dough to a medium bowl. To one half of the dough, add the cherry juice and 3 to 5 drops of the red food coloring. To the other half, add the lime and lemon zest and swirl in 3 to 5 drops of the green food coloring.

Scoop out 1 teaspoon (5 g) of each color of dough and roll each into a ball. Gently squish the balls together and place 2 inches (5 cm) apart on the prepared baking sheets. Repeat the process with the remaining dough. Sprinkle with granulated sugar. Bake in the preheated oven for 9 to 10 minutes, or until golden brown around the bottom edges with no uncooked dough in the centers. Remove from the oven, transfer the cookies to a wire rack and let cool.

ASSEMBLE THE COOKIES
Immediately before serving, place 1 cherry on top of each cooked cookie.

Dark Roast Coffee Cookies

MAKES 36 COOKIES

One of my favorite simple pleasures is that little kick of energy and motivation I feel after enjoying a cup of coffee. The only thing better is feeling that same kick after eating a coffee-flavored cookie *that also contains gooey chocolate*. This cookie is out-of-this-world amazing. The dark roast coffee and dark chocolate give it a deep, robust flavor that you will fall in love with.

¾ cup (1½ sticks; 167 g) salted butter, softened

1 cup (225 g) dark brown sugar

½ cup (100 g) granulated sugar

1 large egg

1 tsp (5 ml) vanilla extract

3 tbsp (45 ml) brewed dark roast coffee

2 cups (250 g) all-purpose flour

½ cup (55 g) unsweetened dark cocoa powder

1½ tbsp (4 g) instant coffee granules

1½ tsp (7 g) baking soda

1 tsp (6 g) salt

1½ cups (263 g) dark chocolate chips

¼ cup (50 g) turbinado sugar, for sprinkling

Preheat the oven to 350°F (180°C) and line 3 baking sheets with parchment paper. Using a stand mixer fitted with the paddle attachment (or a large mixing bowl with a hand mixer), combine the butter, brown and granulated sugar, egg, vanilla and coffee and beat on medium speed until creamy and free of lumps.

In a separate bowl, combine the flour, cocoa powder, instant coffee granules, baking soda and salt. Mix well. Gradually add to the butter mixture and beat on medium speed until just combined. Stir in the chocolate chips.

Using a medium cookie scoop, place 1½-tablespoon-size (22.5-g) chunks of batter in your hands and roll into balls. Place 2 inches (5 cm) apart on the prepared baking sheets. Press down slightly on each ball and sprinkle with turbinado sugar. Bake in the preheated oven for 9 to 11 minutes, or until the centers of the cookies are cooked through. Remove from the oven, transfer the cookies to a wire rack and let cool.

Margarita Cookies

My husband and I always joke that we should have been born in Mexico. We both love spicy Mexican food and margaritas more than the average American. Dan makes a killer margarita that he has perfected over the years. It is by far my most favorite alcoholic beverage, which is why I was giddy about transforming it into a cookie! Do you know how much fun it is to add tequila to cookie batter? I love the subtle hint of alcohol and the delicious resemblance to its liquid counterpart.

COOKIES

1 cup (2 sticks; 225 g) salted butter, softened

1½ cups (300 g) granulated sugar

2 large eggs

1 tsp (5 ml) vanilla extract

1 tbsp (15 ml) freshly squeezed lime juice

2 tbsp (30 ml) tequila

Zest of 2 limes (about 2 tbsp [19 g])

3 cups (375 g) all-purpose flour

1½ tsp (7 g) baking powder

1 tsp (6 g) margarita salt

3 to 5 drops green food coloring

GLAZE

2 cups (240 g) confectioners' sugar

2 to 4 tbsp (30 to 60 ml) milk

MAKE THE COOKIES

Preheat the oven to 350°F (180°C) and line 3 baking sheets with parchment paper. Using a stand mixer fitted with the paddle attachment (or a large mixing bowl with a hand mixer), combine the butter, granulated sugar, eggs, vanilla, lime juice and tequila and beat on medium speed until creamy and free of lumps. Add the lime zest and mix until just combined.

In a separate bowl, combine the flour, baking powder, margarita salt and food coloring. Mix well. Gradually add to the butter mixture and beat on medium speed until just combined.

Using a medium cookie scoop, place 1½-tablespoon-size (22.5-g) chunks of batter in your hands and roll into balls. Place 2 inches (5 cm) apart on the prepared baking sheets and bake in the preheated oven for 10 to 12 minutes, or until golden brown around the bottom edges with no uncooked dough in the centers. Remove from the oven, transfer the cookies to a wire rack and let cool.

MAKE THE GLAZE

Using a stand mixer fitted with the whisk attachment (or a large mixing bowl with a hand mixer), combine the confectioners' sugar and milk 1 tablespoon (15 ml) at a time until the desired consistency is reached. Beat on medium speed until free of lumps.

ASSEMBLE THE COOKIES

Drizzle the glaze over the tops of the cookies.

Chocolate
White Russian Cookies

Incorporating alcohol into a cookie can be challenging. In this recipe, the flavors of the vodka and coffee-flavored liqueur are noticeable but they do not detract from the other amazing flavors. If you are in the mood for a Chocolate White Russian without the hangover, you have found your match!

COOKIES

½ cup (1 stick; 112 g) salted butter, softened

1 cup (225 g) dark brown sugar

¼ cup (50 g) granulated sugar

1 large egg

2 tbsp (30 ml) coffee-flavored liqueur, such as Kahlúa

3 tbsp (45 ml) vodka

3 tbsp (45 ml) heavy whipping cream

2½ cups (310 g) all-purpose flour

1½ tsp (7 g) baking soda

½ tsp baking powder

1 tsp (6 g) fine sea salt

2 tbsp (7 g) instant coffee granules

1½ cups (263 g) semisweet chocolate chips

GLAZE

3 cups (360 g) confectioners' sugar

¼ cup (28 g) unsweetened cocoa powder

3 tbsp (45 ml) coffee-flavored liqueur, such as Kahlúa

1 to 3 tbsp (15 to 45 ml) milk

TOPPING

Whipped cream

MAKE THE COOKIES

Preheat the oven to 350°F (180°C) and line 3 baking sheets with parchment paper. Using a stand mixer fitted with the paddle attachment (or a large mixing bowl with a hand mixer), combine the butter, brown and granulated sugar, egg, liqueur, vodka and cream and beat on medium speed until creamy and free of lumps.

In a separate bowl, combine the flour, baking soda, baking powder, salt and coffee granules. Mix well. Gradually add to the butter mixture and beat on medium speed until just combined. Stir in the chocolate chips.

Using a medium cookie scoop, place 1½-tablespoon-size (22.5-g) chunks of batter in your hands and roll into balls. Place 2 inches (5 cm) apart on the prepared baking sheets and press down on each ball slightly. Bake in the preheated oven for 10 to 12 minutes, or until the cookies are uniformly puffy. Remove from the oven, transfer the cookies to a wire rack and let cool.

MAKE THE GLAZE

Using a stand mixer fitted with the whisk attachment (or a large mixing bowl with a hand mixer), combine the confectioners' sugar, cocoa powder and liqueur. Add the milk 1 tablespoon (15 ml) at a time until the desired consistency is reached. Beat on medium speed for 2 minutes.

ASSEMBLE THE COOKIES

Drizzle the glaze over the tops of the cookies. Top each cookie with 1 to 2 teaspoons (5 to 10 ml) of whipped cream.

Cherry Cola Cookies

MAKES 30 COOKIES

I remember when Cherry Coke first came out. People raved about it, *oh my gosh* you'd think alcohol had just been invented. I begged my mom to buy a six-pack of those cute mini cans (remember those?) every time we went to the store. The simple addition of cherries to that irresistible Coca-Cola flavor was enough to send the entire country into a frenzy. The cookie version of that drink elicits those same frenzied feelings. I love it when simple things are so good.

1 cup (2 sticks; 225 g) salted butter, softened

1 cup (225 g) dark brown sugar

½ cup (100 g) granulated sugar

1 large egg

1 tsp (5 ml) vanilla extract

1 tsp (5 ml) cola-flavored extract, or 5 tbsp (75 ml) cola soda

2 tbsp (30 ml) liquid from maraschino cherry jar

3 cups (375 g) all-purpose flour

1 tsp (5 g) baking soda

1 tsp (6 g) salt

1 cup (145 g) dried cherries

30 stemless maraschino cherries

Preheat the oven to 350°F (180°C) and line 3 baking sheets with parchment paper. Using a stand mixer fitted with the paddle attachment (or a large mixing bowl with a hand mixer), combine the butter, brown and granulated sugar, egg, vanilla, cola extract and cherry juice and beat on medium speed until creamy.

In a separate bowl, combine the flour, baking soda and salt. Mix well. Gradually add to the butter mixture and mix until just combined. Stir in the dried cherries.

Using a medium cookie scoop, place 1½-tablespoon-size (22.5-g) chunks of batter in your hands and roll into balls. Place 2 inches (5 cm) apart on the prepared baking sheets and bake in the preheated oven for 11 to 13 minutes, or until golden brown around the bottom edges with no uncooked dough in the centers. Remove from the oven, transfer the cookies to a wire rack and let cool. Remove the cookies from the oven and immediately press 1 maraschino cherry into the top center of each cookie.

Apple Cider Cookies

My favorite things about fall include: crisp cool air, fires in the fireplace, scary movies, warm comforting beverages and anything involving apples. Wrap it all together and I'm snuggled on the couch with my cute hubby, a fire at our feet. A scary movie is on TV and we're enjoying steaming hot mugs of apple cider. Pure fall heaven, people! This cookie is that scene wrapped up in a single crisp and delicious bite.

COOKIES

¾ cup (1½ sticks; 167 g) salted butter, softened

1 cup (225 g) light brown sugar

½ cup (100 g) granulated sugar

1 large egg

1 tsp (5 ml) vanilla extract

¼ cup (60 g) apple butter, at room temperature

2 cups (250 g) all-purpose flour

1½ tsp (7 g) baking soda

1 tsp (6 g) fine sea salt

2 tsp (5 g) ground cinnamon

½ tsp ground nutmeg

½ tsp ground cloves

ICING

½ cup (45 g) freeze-dried apple

3 cups (360 g) confectioners' sugar

4 to 6 tbsp (60 to 90 ml) apple cider or juice

TOPPING

2 tsp (5 g) ground cinnamon

MAKE THE COOKIES

Preheat the oven to 350°F (180°C) and line 3 baking sheets with parchment paper. Using a stand mixer fitted with the paddle attachment (or a large mixing bowl with a hand mixer), combine the butter, brown and granulated sugar, egg and vanilla and beat on medium speed until creamy and free of lumps. Add the apple butter and mix until combined.

In a separate bowl, combine the flour, baking soda, salt, cinnamon, nutmeg and cloves. Mix well. Gradually add to the butter mixture and beat on medium speed until just combined.

Using a medium cookie scoop, drop the dough by 1½ tablespoons (22.5 g) 2 inches (5 cm) apart onto the prepared baking sheets. Bake in the preheated oven for 9 to 11 minutes, or until golden brown around the bottom edges with no uncooked dough in the centers. Remove from the oven, transfer the cookies to a wire rack and let cool.

MAKE THE ICING

Place the freeze-dried apples in a coffee grinder or small food processor and grind into a powder.

Using a stand mixer fitted with the whisk attachment (or a large mixing bowl with a hand mixer), combine the apple powder and confectioners' sugar. Add the apple cider 1 tablespoon (15 ml) at a time until the desired consistency is reached. Beat on medium speed until free of lumps.

ASSEMBLE THE COOKIES

Spread the icing on the cookies and sprinkle with cinnamon.

Blueberry Mojito Cookies

MAKES 66 COOKIES

Hold onto your socks, people, because this cookie will blow them straight off your feet. The powdered blueberries hidden in the icing turn it into a deep, magical blue color and the flavor will send you to a cloud located in the middle of blueberry heaven. The small, simple piece of mint that sits atop the cookie will instantly make you think of the delicious mojito that it is impersonating.

COOKIES

1 cup (2 sticks; 225 g) salted butter, softened

1 cup (200 g) granulated sugar

1 large egg

1 tsp (5 ml) rum extract, or 3 tbsp (45 ml) white rum

2 tbsp (30 ml) freshly squeezed lime juice

¼ cup (60 ml) milk

3 cups (375 g) all-purpose flour, plus more for dusting

½ tsp baking powder

1 tsp (6 g) salt

Zest of 1 lime (about 1 tbsp [9 g])

ICING

¼ cup (60 g) freeze-dried blueberries

3 cups confectioners' sugar

4 to 6 tbsp (60 to 90 ml) milk

TOPPING

66 (½" [1.3 cm]) pieces fresh mint

66 fresh blueberries

3 tbsp (36 g) turbinado sugar

MAKE THE COOKIES

Using a stand mixer fitted with the paddle attachment (or a large mixing bowl with a hand mixer), combine the butter, granulated sugar, egg, rum extract, lime juice and milk and beat on medium speed until creamy and free of lumps.

In a separate bowl, combine the flour, baking powder and salt. Mix well. Gradually add to the butter mixture and beat on medium speed until just combined. Add the lime zest and mix until just combined.

Place the dough on a large piece of plastic wrap. Wrap the edges around the dough to form a ball and refrigerate for 1 hour.

Preheat the oven to 350°F (180°C) and line 3 baking sheets with parchment paper. Remove the dough from the fridge and sprinkle a flat work surface with flour. Using a rolling pin, roll out the dough to ¼-inch (6-mm) thickness. Using a 2½-inch (6.5-cm) round cookie cutter, cut circles from the dough. Place 1 inch (2.5 cm) apart on the prepared baking sheets and bake in the preheated oven for 7 to 8 minutes, or until the edges are very lightly golden. Remove from the oven, transfer the cookies to a wire rack and let cool. Repeat the rolling and baking process with the remaining dough.

MAKE THE ICING

Place the freeze-dried blueberries in a coffee grinder or small food processor and grind into a powder.

Using a stand mixer fitted with the whisk attachment (or a large mixing bowl with a hand mixer), combine the blueberry powder and confectioners' sugar. Add the milk 1 tablespoon (15 ml) at a time until the desired consistency is reached. Beat on medium speed until free of lumps.

ASSEMBLE THE COOKIES

Spread the icing on the cookies and top each cookie with 1 piece of mint and 1 blueberry. Sprinkle the tops with turbinado sugar.

Blackberry Ice Cream Soda Cookies

Biting into this cookie makes me feel as if I am ten years old, sitting in an ice cream parlor with my dad on a sunny summer Sunday. I chose blackberries for this recipe because it is my favorite berry to enjoy with vanilla ice cream. They make these cookies unique and delicious, and their incredible color creates a sense of otherworldliness.

COOKIES
¾ cup (1½ sticks; 167 g) salted butter, softened

1½ cups (300 g) granulated sugar

2 large eggs

1 tsp (5 ml) vanilla extract

2 tbsp (40 g) blackberry jam

½ cup (120 ml) heavy whipping cream

2½ cups (310 g) all-purpose flour

½ tsp baking soda

1 tsp (5 g) baking powder

1 tsp (6 g) salt

1 cup (145 g) chopped fresh blackberries

FROSTING
½ cup (1 stick; 112 g) salted butter, softened

3 cups (360 g) confectioners' sugar

1 tsp butter extract

½ tsp blackberry extract (optional)

2 tbsp (40 g) blackberry jam

1 to 2 tbsp (15 to 30 ml) milk

Red and blue food coloring

TOPPING
42 fresh blackberries

MAKE THE COOKIES
Preheat the oven to 350°F (180°C) and line 3 baking sheets with parchment paper. Using a stand mixer fitted with the paddle attachment (or a large mixing bowl with a hand mixer), combine the butter, granulated sugar, eggs, vanilla and blackberry jam and beat on medium speed until creamy and free of lumps. Add the cream and mix until smooth.

In a separate bowl, combine the flour, baking soda, baking powder and salt. Mix well. Gradually add to the butter mixture and beat on medium speed until just combined. Fold in the fresh blackberries.

Using a medium cookie scoop, drop the dough by 1½ tablespoons (22.5 g) 2 inches (5 cm) apart onto the prepared baking sheets. Bake in the preheated oven for 9 to 11 minutes, or until golden brown around the bottom edges with no uncooked dough in the centers. Remove from the oven, transfer the cookies to a wire rack and let cool.

MAKE THE FROSTING
Using a stand mixer fitted with the whisk attachment (or a large mixing bowl with a hand mixer), combine the butter, confectioners' sugar, butter extract, blackberry extract (if using) and blackberry jam. Add the milk 1 tablespoon (15 ml) at a time until the desired consistency is reached. Beat on medium speed for 3 minutes. Add the red and blue food coloring and mix until a light purple color is even throughout.

ASSEMBLE THE COOKIES
Spread the frosting on the cookies and top each cookie with 1 blackberry.

Earl Grey Lemon Tea Cookies

MAKES 95 COOKIES

There is a brilliant little secret hidden in this recipe, shared with me by my friend Jane who is an incredibly talented baker. Steeping Earl Grey tea in the milk that goes into the frosting is a genius way to add the flavor of tea into the cookie without overpowering it. I love the many facets of this cookie. It makes me feel as if I'm drinking a cup of lemon Earl Grey tea, except with much more indulgence.

COOKIES

1 cup (2 sticks; 225 g) salted butter, softened

1 cup (200 g) granulated sugar

1 large egg

1 tsp (5 ml) lemon extract, or 1 tbsp (9 g) additional lemon zest

¼ cup (60 ml) milk

3 cups (375 g) all-purpose flour, plus more for dusting

½ tsp baking powder

½ tsp salt

Zest of 1 lemon (about 1 tbsp [9 g])

ICING

¼ cup (60 ml) warm milk

1 Earl Grey tea bag

2 cups (240 g) confectioners' sugar

1 tsp (5 ml) lemon extract

TOPPING

Lemon zest and/or yellow sugar sprinkles

MAKE THE COOKIES

Using a stand mixer fitted with the paddle attachment (or a large mixing bowl with a hand mixer), combine the butter, granulated sugar, egg, lemon extract (or lemon zest) and milk and beat on medium speed until creamy and free of lumps.

In a separate bowl, combine the flour, baking powder and salt. Mix well. Gradually add to the butter mixture and beat on medium speed until just combined. Add the lemon zest and mix until just combined.

Place the dough on a large piece of plastic wrap. Wrap the edges around the dough to form a ball and refrigerate for 1 hour.

Preheat the oven to 350°F (180°C) and line 3 baking sheets with parchment paper. Remove the dough from the fridge and sprinkle a flat work surface with flour. Using a rolling pin, roll out the dough to ¼-inch (6-mm) thickness. Using a 1½-inch (4-cm) round cookie cutter, cut circles from the dough. Place 1 inch (2.5 cm) apart on the prepared baking sheets and bake in the preheated oven for 7 to 8 minutes, or until the edges are very lightly golden. Remove from the oven, transfer the cookies to a wire rack and let cool. Repeat the rolling and baking process with the remaining dough.

MAKE THE ICING

Pour the milk into a small mug and add the tea bag. Cover the mug and let steep for 10 minutes.

Using a stand mixer fitted with the whisk attachment (or a large mixing bowl with a hand mixer), combine the confectioners' sugar and lemon extract. Remove the tea bag from the milk and pour the milk into the sugar mixture. Beat on medium speed until free of lumps.

ASSEMBLE THE COOKIES

Spread the icing on the cookies and top each cookie with lemon zest and/or sprinkles.

Raspberry Lemonade Cookies

MAKES 32 COOKIES

I find the combination of raspberries and lemons to be insanely satisfying and refreshing. Every part of this cookie is incredible, from the intense raspberry flavoring in the cookie to the lemony glaze and candied lemon slice. It is also the prettiest cookie you'll ever eat!

CANDIED LEMON SLICES

1 cup (200 g) granulated sugar

2 tbsp (30 ml) freshly squeezed lemon juice

2 lemons, sliced to ⅛-inch (3-mm) thickness

COOKIES

¾ cup (1½ sticks; 167 g) salted butter, softened

1½ cups (300 g) granulated sugar

1 large egg

1 tsp (5 ml) lemon extract

¼ cup (8 g) freeze-dried raspberries

2 cups (250 g) all-purpose flour

1 tsp (5 g) baking powder

1 tsp (6 g) salt

Zest of 1 lemon (about 1 tbsp [9 g])

1 tbsp (15 ml) freshly squeezed lemon juice

1 cup (125 g) chopped fresh raspberries

GLAZE

2 cups (240 g) confectioners' sugar

1 tsp (5 ml) lemon extract

2 tbsp (30 ml) freshly squeezed lemon juice

2 tbsp (30 ml) milk

MAKE THE CANDIED LEMON SLICES

In a large heavy-duty saucepan, combine the granulated sugar, lemon juice and 1 cup (235 ml) of water. Bring the mixture to a boil over medium-high heat. Lower to medium-low and add the lemon slices in a single layer. Simmer for 15 minutes, or until the lemon slices turn a deep yellow color, gently flipping them once or twice during the cooking process. Transfer the lemon slices to a wire cooling rack and allow them to cool completely.

MAKE THE COOKIES

Preheat the oven to 350°F (180°C) and line 3 baking sheets with parchment paper. Using a stand mixer fitted with the paddle attachment (or a large mixing bowl with a hand mixer), combine the butter, granulated sugar, egg and lemon extract and beat on medium speed until creamy and free of lumps.

Place the freeze-dried raspberries in a coffee grinder or small food processor and grind into a powder. In a separate bowl, combine the raspberry powder, flour, baking powder and salt. Mix well. Gradually add to the butter mixture and beat on medium speed until just combined. Add the lemon zest and lemon juice and mix until just combined. Fold in the fresh raspberries. Using a medium cookie scoop, drop the dough by 1½ tablespoons (22.5 g) 2 inches (5 cm) apart onto the prepared baking sheets. Bake in the preheated oven for 9 to 11 minutes, or until golden brown around the bottom edges with no uncooked dough in the centers. Remove from the oven, transfer the cookies to a wire rack and let cool.

MAKE THE GLAZE

Using a stand mixer fitted with the whisk attachment (or a large mixing bowl with a hand mixer), combine the confectioners' sugar, lemon extract, lemon juice and milk. Beat on medium speed until free of lumps.

ASSEMBLE THE COOKIES

Generously drizzle the glaze over the cookies. Top each cookie with half of a cooled candied lemon slice.

Chocolate Macchiato Cookies

MAKES 34 COOKIES

This cookie ranks in the top three for being most memorable during recipe testing. Months later, friends are still asking me, "Remember those delicious cookies you made? When are you going to make more?" Close your eyes when you sink your teeth in and you will think you just took a sip of an irresistible chocolate macchiato.

COOKIES

¾ cup (1½ sticks; 167 g) salted butter, softened

1 cup (225 g) dark brown sugar

½ cup (100 g) granulated sugar

1 large egg

1 tsp (5 ml) vanilla extract

¼ cup (60 ml) chocolate liqueur

2½ cups (310 g) all-purpose flour

⅓ cup (37 g) unsweetened cocoa powder

1 tbsp (3 g) instant coffee granules

1 tsp (5 g) baking soda

½ tsp baking powder

1 tsp (6 g) salt

1 cup (175 g) semisweet chocolate chips

FROSTING

1 (3.5-oz [100-g]) package instant chocolate pudding mix

1 (8-oz [225-g]) container whipped topping, thawed

½ cup (60 g) confectioners' sugar

½ cup (120 ml) heavy whipping cream

TOPPING

Chocolate syrup

MAKE THE COOKIES

Preheat the oven to 350°F (180°C) and line 3 baking sheets with parchment paper. Using a stand mixer fitted with the paddle attachment (or a large mixing bowl with a hand mixer), combine the butter, brown and granulated sugar, egg, vanilla and chocolate liqueur and beat on medium speed until creamy and free of lumps.

In a separate bowl, combine the flour, cocoa powder, coffee granules, baking soda, baking powder and salt. Mix well. Gradually add to the butter mixture and beat on medium speed until just combined. Stir in the chocolate chips until combined.

Using a medium cookie scoop, place 1½-tablespoon-size (22.5 g) chunks of batter in your hands and roll into balls. Place 2 inches (5 cm) apart on the prepared baking sheets. Bake in the preheated oven for 10 to 11 minutes, or until the centers of the cookies are cooked through. Remove from the oven, transfer the cookies to a wire rack and let cool.

MAKE THE FROSTING

Using a stand mixer fitted with the whisk attachment (or a large mixing bowl with a hand mixer), combine the pudding mix, whipped topping, confectioners' sugar and cream. Beat on medium speed for 3 minutes.

ASSEMBLE THE COOKIES

Generously spread the frosting on the cookies. Drizzle with chocolate syrup. Refrigerate until ready to serve.

Moscow Mule Cookies

MAKES 37 COOKIES

Moscow Mules are trendy for good reason. Ginger and lime create such an unexpected zingy freshness that it is almost breathtaking. Everything enjoyable about the drink is also enjoyable in the cookie. The flavors will hit your taste buds at slightly different times and suddenly you'll have a mouthful of the drink-turned-cookie. This cookie is a huge hit with adults, whether they're familiar with the popular beverage or not.

COOKIES

¾ cup (1½ sticks; 167 g) salted butter, softened

1½ cups (300 g) granulated sugar

1 large egg

1 tsp (5 ml) vanilla extract

2 tbsp (15 ml) vodka

5 tbsp (75 ml) ginger beer, at room temperature

2½ cups (310 g) all-purpose flour

½ tsp baking soda

1 tsp (5 g) baking powder

1 tsp (6 g) fine sea salt

2 tsp (4 g) ground ginger

GLAZE

3 cups (360 g) confectioners' sugar

Zest of 1 lime (about 1 tbsp [9 g])

4 to 6 tbsp (60 to 90 ml) freshly squeezed lime juice

MAKE THE COOKIES

Preheat the oven to 350°F (180°C) and line 3 baking sheets with parchment paper. Using a stand mixer fitted with the paddle attachment (or a large mixing bowl with a hand mixer), combine the butter, granulated sugar, egg, vanilla, vodka and ginger beer and beat on medium speed until creamy and free of lumps.

In a separate bowl, combine the flour, baking soda, baking powder, salt and ginger. Mix well. Gradually add to the butter mixture and beat on medium speed until just combined.

Using a medium cookie scoop, drop the dough by 1½ tablespoons (22.5 g) 2 inches (5 cm) apart onto the prepared baking sheets. Bake in the preheated oven for 9 to 11 minutes, or until golden brown around the bottom edges with no uncooked dough in the centers. Remove from the oven, transfer the cookies to a wire rack and let cool.

MAKE THE GLAZE

Using a stand mixer fitted with the whisk attachment (or a large mixing bowl with a hand mixer), combine the confectioners' sugar and lime zest. Add the lime juice 1 tablespoon (15 ml) at a time until the desired consistency is reached. Beat on medium speed until free of lumps.

ASSEMBLE THE COOKIES

Drizzle the glaze over the cookies.

Eggnog Cookies

MAKES 44 COOKIES

Around Christmastime every year, all of my boys enjoy indulging in eggnog. If you were to describe the drink to me, I would tell you it sounds fantastic. But when I take an actual sip, I don't love it. I was hesitant to turn it into a cookie for this reason, but was so pleasantly surprised to discover that the cookie version of the creamy holiday beverage is totally irresistible!

COOKIES

¾ cup (1½ sticks; 167 g) salted butter, softened

1 cup (225 g) light brown sugar

½ cup (100 g) granulated sugar

1 large egg

1 tsp (5 ml) vanilla extract

2 tsp (10 ml) rum extract

2 cups (250 g) all-purpose flour

1 tsp (5 g) baking soda

½ tsp baking powder

1 tsp (6 g) fine sea salt

1 tsp (2 g) ground cinnamon

½ tsp ground nutmeg

¼ tsp ground cloves

2 tbsp (28 g) eggnog mix, or ½ cup (120 ml) eggnog

FROSTING

½ cup (1 stick; 112 g) salted butter, softened

3 cups (360 g) confectioners' sugar

2 tbsp (28 g) eggnog mix plus 1 to 3 tbsp (15 to 45 ml) milk, or 3 to 6 tbsp (45 to 90 ml) eggnog

TOPPING

Ground cinnamon and/or nutmeg

MAKE THE COOKIES

Preheat the oven to 350°F (180°C) and line 3 baking sheets with parchment paper. Using a stand mixer fitted with the paddle attachment (or a large mixing bowl with a hand mixer), combine the butter, brown and granulated sugar, egg, vanilla and rum extract and beat on medium speed until creamy and free of lumps.

In a separate bowl, combine the flour, baking soda, baking powder, salt, cinnamon, nutmeg, cloves and eggnog mix. Mix well. Gradually add to the butter mixture and beat on medium speed until just combined.

Scoop out tablespoon-size (15-g) chunks of batter and form balls, using your hands. Place 2 inches (5 cm) apart on the prepared baking sheets. Bake in the preheated oven for 9 to 11 minutes, or until golden brown around the bottom edges with no uncooked dough in the centers. Remove from the oven, transfer the cookies to a wire rack and let cool.

MAKE THE FROSTING

Using a stand mixer fitted with the whisk attachment (or a large mixing bowl with a hand mixer), combine the butter, confectioners' sugar and eggnog mix. Add the milk 1 tablespoon (15 ml) at a time until the desired consistency is reached. Beat on medium speed for 3 minutes.

ASSEMBLE THE COOKIES

Spread the frosting on the cookies and sprinkle each cookie with cinnamon and/or nutmeg.

> **NOTE:** Use 2½ cups (310 g) of flour if using eggnog instead of eggnog mix when making the cookies.

Strawberry Milkshake Cookies

I would choose strawberry milkshakes over chocolate or vanilla any day of the week. The little chunks of strawberries make it extra fun and exciting. It is my favorite flavor of milkshake by far, which is why I love this cookie so dearly. It is infused with intense strawberry flavor, thanks to the freeze-dried fruit!

½ cup (1 stick; 112 g) salted butter, softened

½ cup (115 g) light brown sugar

1 cup (200 g) granulated sugar

1 large egg

1 tsp (5 ml) vanilla extract

3 tbsp (45 g) vanilla yogurt

¼ cup (8 g) freeze-dried strawberries

2½ cups (310 g) all-purpose flour

1 tbsp (7 g) original malted milk powder

½ tsp baking soda

1 tsp (5 g) baking powder

1 tsp (6 g) fine sea salt

¾ cup (128 g) chopped fresh strawberries, patted dry

Preheat the oven to 350°F (180°C) and line 3 baking sheets with parchment paper. Using a stand mixer fitted with the paddle attachment (or a large mixing bowl with a hand mixer), combine the butter, brown and granulated sugar, egg, vanilla and yogurt and beat on medium speed until creamy and free of lumps.

Place the freeze-dried strawberries in a coffee grinder or small food processor and grind into a powder.

In a separate bowl, combine the strawberry powder, flour, malted milk powder, baking soda, baking powder and salt. Mix well. Gradually add to the butter mixture and beat on medium speed until just combined. Fold in the fresh strawberries.

Using a medium cookie scoop, drop the dough by 1½ tablespoons (22.5 g) 2 inches (5 cm) apart onto the prepared baking sheets. Bake in the preheated oven for 9 to 11 minutes, or until golden brown around the bottom edges with no uncooked dough in the centers. Remove from the oven, transfer the cookies to a wire rack and let cool.

Blackberry Green Tea Cookies

MAKES 38 COOKIES

I'm begging you not to read the words *green tea* and become bored out of your gourd. Tea is often subtly flavored (a tad boring), but when it is paired with blackberries and sugar, it reaches mind-blowing status. These cookies explode with delightful little bursts of flavor inside your mouth. Cater the amount of tea used in the recipe to your liking, but I find perfection in the amount in the recipe. It does not overpower the other ingredients, yet it is noticeable and perfectly scrumptious.

¼ cup (60 ml) warm milk

1 green tea with matcha tea bag, plus 2 tbsp (9 g) loose tea (removed from tea bags)

¾ cup (1½ sticks; 167 g) salted butter, softened

1 cup (225 g) light brown sugar

½ cup (100 g) granulated sugar

1 large egg

1 tsp (5 ml) vanilla extract

2½ cups (310 g) all-purpose flour

1 tsp (5 g) baking soda

½ tsp baking powder

1 tsp (6 g) salt

Green food coloring, if desired

2 cups (290 g) fresh blackberries, chopped

38 fresh blackberries, for topping

Pour the milk into a small mug and add the green tea bag. Cover the mug and let steep for 10 minutes.

Preheat the oven to 350°F (180°C) and line 3 baking sheets with parchment paper. Using a stand mixer fitted with the paddle attachment (or a large mixing bowl with a hand mixer), combine the butter, brown and granulated sugar, egg and vanilla and beat on medium speed until creamy and free of lumps.

Place the 2 tablespoons (9 g) of loose green tea in a coffee grinder or small food processor and grind into a powder.

In a separate bowl, combine the green tea powder, flour, baking soda, baking powder and salt. Mix well. Gradually add to the butter mixture and beat on medium speed until just combined.

Remove the tea bag from the milk and pour the milk into the butter mixture. Mix until just combined. Swirl in food coloring, if desired. Fold in the chopped blackberries.

Using a medium cookie scoop, drop the dough by 1½ tablespoons (22.5 g) 2 inches (5 cm) apart onto the prepared baking sheets. Bake in the preheated oven for 10 to 12 minutes, or until golden brown around the bottom edges with no uncooked dough in the centers. Remove from the oven, transfer the cookies to a wire rack and let cool. Top each cookie with 1 blackberry.

Limoncello Cookies

There is something magical about the freshness of lemons, which explains why I've always swooned over limoncello. Just seeing a bottle of the yellow nectar makes me giddy. When I started writing this book, I knew limoncello had to be involved. Simply put, turning it into a cookie was fun, tasty and life-altering.

COOKIES

¾ cup (1½ sticks; 167 g) salted butter, softened

1 cup (200 g) granulated sugar

½ cup (60 g) confectioners' sugar

1 large egg

1 tsp (5 ml) lemon extract, or 1 tbsp (9 g) additional lemon zest

¼ cup (60 ml) limoncello liqueur

Zest of 1 lemon (about 1 tbsp [9 g])

2 cups (250 g) all-purpose flour

1 tsp (5 g) baking powder

1 tsp (6 g) salt

ICING

2 cups (120 g) confectioners' sugar

1 tbsp (15 ml) freshly squeezed lemon juice

TOPPING

Yellow and/or white sugar sprinkles

MAKE THE COOKIES

Preheat the oven to 350°F (180°C) and line 3 baking sheets with parchment paper. Using a stand mixer fitted with the paddle attachment (or a large mixing bowl with a hand mixer), combine the butter, granulated and confectioners' sugar, egg, lemon extract, limoncello and lemon zest and beat on medium speed until creamy and free of lumps.

In a separate bowl, combine the flour, baking powder and salt. Mix well. Gradually add to the butter mixture and beat on medium speed until just combined.

Using a medium cookie scoop, drop the dough by 1½ tablespoons (22.5 g) 2 inches (5 cm) apart onto the prepared baking sheets. Bake in the preheated oven for 9 to 11 minutes, or until golden brown around the bottom edges with no uncooked dough in the centers. Remove from the oven, transfer the cookies to a wire rack and let cool.

MAKE THE ICING

Using a stand mixer fitted with the whisk attachment (or a large mixing bowl with a hand mixer), combine the confectioners' sugar and lemon juice. Beat on medium speed until free of lumps.

ASSEMBLE THE COOKIES

Spread the icing on the cookies and top each cookie with sprinkles as desired.

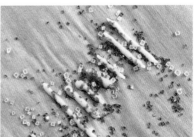

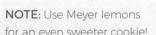
NOTE: Use Meyer lemons for an even sweeter cookie!

Tropical Fruit Smoothie Cookies

MAKES 40 COOKIES

I mentally squeal any time the word *tropical* describes food or drink. Tropical equals carefree, fresh, exotic, fun and colorful. All of these words perfectly describe this smoothie-turned-cookie. The only thing that would make it better would be to eat it while sitting on a tropical beach.

COOKIES

¾ cup (1½ sticks; 167 g) salted butter, softened

1½ cups (300 g) granulated sugar

1 large egg

1 tsp (5 ml) orange extract

¼ cup (8 g) freeze-dried mango

¼ cup (8 g) freeze-dried pineapple

2 cups (250 g) all-purpose flour

½ tsp baking soda

1 tsp (5 g) baking powder

1 tsp (6 g) salt

FROSTING

½ cup (1 stick; 112 g) salted butter, softened

3 cups (360 g) confectioners' sugar

1 tsp (5 ml) orange extract

Zest of 1 orange (about 1 tbsp [9 g])

1 to 3 tbsp (15 to 45 ml) freshly squeezed orange juice

TOPPING

Zest of 1 orange

MAKE THE COOKIES

Preheat the oven to 350°F (180°C) and line 3 baking sheets with parchment paper. Using a stand mixer fitted with the paddle attachment (or a large mixing bowl with a hand mixer), combine the butter, granulated sugar, egg and orange extract and beat on medium speed until creamy and free of lumps.

Place the freeze-dried mango and pineapple in a coffee grinder or small food processor and grind into a powder.

In a separate bowl, combine the mango and pineapple powder, flour, baking soda, baking powder and salt. Mix well. Gradually add to the butter mixture and beat on medium speed until just combined.

Scoop out tablespoon-size (15-g) chunks of batter and form balls, using your hands. Place 2 inches (5 cm) apart on the prepared baking sheets. Bake in the preheated oven for 9 to 11 minutes, or until golden brown around the bottom edges with no uncooked dough in the centers. Remove from the oven, transfer the cookies to a wire rack and let cool.

MAKE THE FROSTING

Using a stand mixer fitted with the whisk attachment (or a large mixing bowl with a hand mixer), combine the butter, confectioners' sugar, orange extract and orange zest. Add the orange juice 1 tablespoon (15 ml) at a time until the desired consistency is reached. Beat on medium speed for 3 minutes.

ASSEMBLE THE COOKIES

Spread the frosting on the cookies and top each cookie with additional orange zest.

Salted Caramel Latte Cookies

MAKES 27 COOKIES

It wasn't until a few years ago that I became a coffee drinker. I once believed that coffee came in a single boring flavor. I've since learned that there is an entire world of coffee to explore! My current favorite variety is the salted caramel latte and I absolutely love the cookie version of the caffeinated beverage. It tastes just like the drink and it even comes with a bonus caffeine kick. This one is for caffeine-loving adults only!

¾ cup (1½ sticks; 167 g) salted butter, softened

⅔ cup (170 g) dark brown sugar

⅓ cup (65 g) granulated sugar

1 large egg

1 tsp (5 ml) vanilla extract

2½ cups (310 g) all-purpose flour

1 tbsp (3 g) medium roast coffee granules

½ tsp baking soda

1½ tsp (7 g) baking powder

1 tsp (6 g) salt

3 tbsp (45 ml) milk

1 (11-oz [310-g]) package caramel bits

Coarse sea salt, for sprinkling

Preheat the oven to 350°F (180°C) and line 2 baking sheets with parchment paper. Using a stand mixer fitted with the paddle attachment (or a large mixing bowl with a hand mixer), combine the butter, brown and granulated sugar, egg and vanilla and beat on medium speed until creamy and free of lumps.

In a separate bowl, combine the flour, coffee granules, baking soda, baking powder and salt. Mix well. Gradually add to the butter mixture and beat on medium speed until just combined. Add the milk and beat until just combined. Fold in the caramel bits.

Using a medium cookie scoop, drop the dough by 1½ tablespoons (22.5 g) 2 inches (5 cm) apart onto the prepared baking sheets. Bake in the preheated oven for 12 to 13 minutes, or until golden brown around the bottom edges with no uncooked dough in the centers. Remove from the oven, transfer the cookies to a wire rack and let cool. Immediately sprinkle sea salt over the tops.

Pumpkin Spice Latte Cookies

MAKES 38 COOKIES

Alternate title: The Cookie That Transformed a Pumpkin Hater into a Pumpkin Lover.
I offered one of these cookies to a friend and she politely declined. "No, thanks, I don't care for pumpkin," she said. I insisted and she reluctantly tried a bite. Then the entire cookie was gone. And then she started on the next. This isn't your typical pumpkin cookie, people, and it tastes so much like a pumpkin spice latte that the chewing becomes sort of confusing.

COOKIES
¾ cup (1½ sticks; 167 g) salted butter, softened

1 cup (225 g) dark brown sugar

½ cup (100 g) granulated sugar, plus 2 tbsp (25 g), for sprinkling, divided

1 large egg

2 tsp (10 ml) vanilla extract

½ cup (123 g) pure pumpkin puree

2½ cups (310 g) all-purpose flour

2 tbsp (7 g) medium roast coffee granules

1½ tsp (7 g) baking soda

½ tsp baking powder

1 tsp (6 g) fine sea salt

1 tsp (3 g) pumpkin pie spice

GLAZE
3 cups (360 g) confectioners' sugar

1 tsp (3 g) pumpkin pie spice

3 to 5 tbsp (45 to 75 ml) milk

TOPPING
Sugar sprinkles

Whipped cream

Pumpkin pie spice

MAKE THE COOKIES
Preheat the oven to 350°F (180°C) and line 3 baking sheets with parchment paper. Using a stand mixer fitted with the paddle attachment (or a large mixing bowl with a hand mixer), combine the butter, brown and granulated sugar, egg, vanilla and pumpkin and beat on medium speed until creamy and free of lumps.

In a separate bowl, combine the flour, coffee granules, baking soda, baking powder, salt and pumpkin pie spice. Mix well. Gradually add to the butter mixture and beat on medium speed until just combined.

Using a medium cookie scoop, drop the dough by 1½ tablespoons (22.5 g) 2 inches (5 cm) apart onto the prepared baking sheets. Sprinkle granulated sugar over the tops. Bake in the preheated oven for 9 to 11 minutes, or until golden brown around the bottom edges with no uncooked dough in the centers. Remove from the oven, transfer the cookies to a wire rack and let cool.

MAKE THE GLAZE
Using a stand mixer fitted with the whisk attachment (or a large mixing bowl with a hand mixer), combine the confectioners' sugar and pumpkin pie spice. Add the milk 1 tablespoon (15 ml) at a time until the desired consistency is reached. Beat on medium speed until free of lumps.

ASSEMBLE THE COOKIES
Drizzle the glaze over the cookies and top with sugar sprinkles, a squirt of whipped cream and a sprinkling of pumpkin pie spice.

Chai Tea Cookies

Most tea makes me yawn, but not the robust and complicated chai. Taking a sip of chai tea is like experiencing a fireworks finale inside the confines of my mouth. There are times when too many cooks in the kitchen is a bad thing, but not with the cookie formed after this complexly delicious tea. I *love* experiencing these powerhouse flavors together in a single bite.

¾ cup (1½ sticks; 167 g) salted butter, softened

1 cup (225 g) light brown sugar

½ cup (100 g) granulated sugar

1 large egg

1 tsp (5 ml) vanilla extract

1 tbsp (5 g) loose chai tea (removed from tea bags)

2½ cups (310 g) all-purpose flour

1 tsp (5 g) baking soda

½ tsp baking powder

1 tsp (6 g) fine sea salt

½ tsp ground cinnamon

¼ tsp ground ginger

¼ tsp ground cardamom

¼ tsp ground cloves

¼ cup (60 ml) milk

½ cup (100 g) turbinado sugar

Preheat the oven to 350°F (180°C) and line 3 baking sheets with parchment paper. Using a stand mixer fitted with the paddle attachment (or a large mixing bowl with a hand mixer), combine the butter, brown and granulated sugar, egg and vanilla and beat on medium speed until creamy and free of lumps.

Place the loose chai tea in a coffee grinder or small food processor and grind into a powder.

In a separate bowl, combine the chai tea powder, flour, baking soda, baking powder, salt, cinnamon, ginger, cardamom and cloves. Mix well. Gradually add to the butter mixture and beat on medium speed until just combined. Add the milk and mix until creamy.

Scoop out tablespoon-size (15-g) chunks of batter and form balls, using your hands. Roll the balls in the turbinado sugar to coat completely. Place 2 inches (5 cm) apart on the prepared baking sheets. Bake in the preheated oven for 8 to 10 minutes, or until golden brown around the bottom edges with no uncooked dough in the centers. Remove from the oven, transfer the cookies to a wire rack and let cool.

Rum Punch Cookies

MAKES 32 COOKIES

Rum punch makes me think of Jamaica, catamaran cruises, suntans, snorkeling, warm sunny beaches and carefree joy. I don't know any other two words that provoke such instant gratifying simultaneous thoughts. I created this cookie with all of that dreaminess in mind all while imagining the Jamaican winds blowing through my hair. The cookie has an uncanny resemblance to the drink. If only I could open my eyes and be on a Jamaican beach!

¾ cup (1½ sticks; 167 g) salted butter, softened

½ cup (115 g) light brown sugar

1 cup (200 g) granulated sugar

1 large egg

1 tsp (5 ml) rum extract

2 tbsp (30 ml) dark rum

2 tbsp (30 ml) grenadine

Zest of 2 oranges (about 2 tbsp [19 g])

3 cups (375 g) all-purpose flour

½ tsp baking soda

1 tsp (5 g) baking powder

1 tsp (6 g) salt

2 large eggs, beaten

1 cup (85 g) sweetened coconut flakes

Preheat the oven to 350°F (180°C) and line 3 baking sheets with parchment paper. Using a stand mixer fitted with the paddle attachment (or a large mixing bowl with a hand mixer), combine the butter, brown and granulated sugar, egg, rum extract, rum and grenadine and beat on medium speed until creamy and free of lumps. Add the orange zest and mix until just combined.

In a separate bowl, combine the flour, baking soda, baking powder and salt. Mix well. Gradually add to the butter mixture and beat on medium speed until just combined.

Whisk the eggs in a small bowl and place the coconut flakes in another small bowl. Using a medium cookie scoop, place 1½-tablespoon-size (22.5-g) chunks of batter in your hands and roll into balls. Roll each ball first in the beaten eggs, followed by the coconut flakes, coating completely.

Place 2 inches (5 cm) apart on the prepared baking sheets and bake in the preheated oven for 10 to 12 minutes, or until golden brown around the bottom edges with no uncooked dough in the centers. Remove from the oven, transfer the cookies to a wire rack and let cool.

NOTE: Grenadine is found most easily at liquor stores in the mixers section.

Chocolate Banana Malt Cookies

MAKES 32 COOKIES

When I envision a chocolate banana malt in my mind, I begin to feel slightly overwhelmed. There are so many different flavors involved that it seems impossible to capture tastes from every aspect in a single sip. This cookie is the perfect solution because that ideal combination of flavors hits the taste buds at the same time.

¾ cup (1½ sticks; 167 g) salted butter, softened

1 cup (225 g) light brown sugar

½ cup (100 g) granulated sugar

1 large egg

1 tsp (5 ml) vanilla extract

1½ cups (185 g) all-purpose flour

½ cup (55 g) unsweetened cocoa powder

¼ cup (33 g) chocolate malted milk powder

1½ tsp (7 g) baking soda

1 tbsp (8 g) cornstarch

1 tsp (6 g) salt

2 ripe bananas, mashed

1 cup (175 g) milk chocolate chips

Preheat the oven to 350°F (180°C) and line 3 baking sheets with parchment paper. Using a stand mixer fitted with the paddle attachment (or a large mixing bowl with a hand mixer), combine the butter, brown and granulated sugar, egg and vanilla and beat on medium speed until creamy and free of lumps.

In a separate bowl, combine the flour, cocoa powder, malted milk powder, baking soda, cornstarch and salt. Mix well. Gradually add to the butter mixture and beat on medium speed until just combined. Stir in the bananas and chocolate chips until just combined.

Using a medium cookie scoop, drop the dough by 1½ tablespoons (22.5 g) 2 inches (5 cm) apart onto the prepared baking sheets. Bake in the preheated oven for 10 to 11 minutes, or until golden brown around the bottom edges with no uncooked dough in the centers. Remove from the oven, transfer the cookies to a wire rack and let cool.

NOTE: Malted milk powder can be found in the grocery store near the ice cream cones/toppings.

Peppermint
Hot Chocolate Cookies

MAKES 22 COOKIES

My boys insist on drinking hot chocolate every single time they come in from playing in the snow. Sometimes I think it's the only reason they go outside! Of course, marshmallows always have to be involved, and I've recently started branching out and adding other flavors, such as peppermint. Sammy and I both love the peppermint version of the winter beverage and this cookie is an exact replica of it.

¾ cup (1½ sticks; 167 g) salted butter, softened

1½ cups (300 g) granulated sugar

2 large eggs

2 tsp (10 ml) peppermint extract

2¼ cups (280 g) all-purpose flour

½ cup (55 g) unsweetened cocoa powder

¼ tsp baking soda

2 tsp (9 g) baking powder

1 tsp (6 g) salt

1½ cups (75 g) miniature marshmallows

1½ cups (263 g) milk chocolate chips

½ cup (77 g) crushed peppermint candy canes

Preheat the oven to 350°F (180°C) and line 2 baking sheets with parchment paper. Using a stand mixer fitted with the paddle attachment (or a large mixing bowl with a hand mixer), combine the butter, granulated sugar, eggs and peppermint extract and beat on medium speed until creamy.

In a separate bowl, combine the flour, cocoa powder, baking soda, baking powder and salt. Mix well. Gradually add to the butter mixture and mix until just combined. Flatten the dough into a disk, wrap in plastic wrap and refrigerate for 2 hours.

Remove the chilled dough from the refrigerator. Scoop out 2 tablespoons (30 g) of dough and flatten into a disk approximately 2½-inches (6.5-cm) in diameter, using your fingers. Place 2 marshmallows and 3 chocolate chips in the center and wrap the dough tightly around it, forming a ball. Smooth out the creases in the dough. Repeat the process with the remaining dough, marshmallows and chocolate chips.

Place 2 inches (5 cm) apart on the prepared baking sheets and bake in the preheated oven for 10 minutes, or until golden brown around the bottom edges with no uncooked dough in the centers. Immediately press 3 chocolate chips and 3 marshmallows into the top of each cookie. Sprinkle with the crushed candy canes.

Shirley Temple Cookies

MAKES 30 COOKIES

There was a restaurant my mom took me to as a kid where I would order a Shirley Temple (or three) to go along with every meal. I couldn't tell you a thing about the food, but I'll never forget enjoying this delicious kid drink and the bonus cherries that came along with it. I enjoy the same things about the cookie. Simplicity wins!

¾ cup (1½ sticks; 167 g) salted butter, softened

1 cup (200 g) granulated sugar

2 large eggs

1 tsp (5 ml) lemon extract

¼ cup (60 ml) grenadine

Zest of 2 limes (about 2 tbsp [19 g])

Zest of 1 lemon (about 1 tbsp [9 g])

2½ cups (310 g) all-purpose flour

1½ tsp (7 g) baking powder

1 tsp (6 g) salt

1 cup (190 g) chopped maraschino cherries, patted dry

Preheat the oven to 350°F (180°C) and line 3 baking sheets with parchment paper. Using a stand mixer fitted with the paddle attachment (or a large mixing bowl with a hand mixer), combine the butter, granulated sugar, eggs, lemon extract and grenadine and beat on medium speed until creamy and free of lumps. Add the lime and lemon zest and mix until just combined.

In a separate bowl, combine the flour, baking powder and salt. Mix well. Gradually add to the butter mixture and beat on medium speed until just combined. Fold in the cherries.

Using a medium cookie scoop, drop the dough by 1½ tablespoons (22.5 g) 2 inches (5 cm) apart onto the prepared baking sheets. Bake in the preheated oven for 9 to 10 minutes, or until golden brown around the bottom edges with no uncooked dough in the centers. Remove from the oven, transfer the cookies to a wire rack and let cool.

NOTE: Grenadine is found most easily at liquor stores in the mixers section.

Cakes and Pies

Cookies inspired by cheesecakes, fruity pies and more!

My family's favorite from this section:

Me: Triple Chocolate Cake Cookies (page 66)—Biting into this cookie was one of the most delicious moments of my life. Everything about this cookie is perfect and fantastic and I don't know that another chocolate cookie could ever beat it.

Hubby Dan: Key Lime Pie Cookies (page 65)—"I love Key lime pie and this cookie was the perfect replica of it."

Elijah (age 10): Black Forest Cake Cookies (page 70)—"This was my most favorite of all! It was so chocolatey and yummy and the cherries made it sizzle."

Sammy (age 7): Cherry Pie Cookies (page 69)—"It actually looked and tasted like a real pie!"

I very seldom make cakes or pies. Even on birthdays I usually make cupcakes because it seems like the easy thing to do. The thought of making an entire actual pie stresses me out. In addition to the painstaking effort involved, who will eat it all? Unless a major holiday is approaching, pie-making does not even enter my thoughts. And even then it's a flittering thought that vanishes instantly.

But, cakes and pies are so yummy! They need to be enjoyed! Which is why you absolutely *need* to make every cookie within this delicious section. Enjoying cakes and pies without the hassle and in just a few bites is a delicious dream come true.

Key Lime Pie Cookies

MAKES 36 COOKIES

Key limes. They're so little and cute that I could just pinch their cheeks. In case you're not familiar with Key limes, they are smaller and more acidic than the more popular Persian lime. They are known for having a unique flavor that pairs well with baking. The famous pie is called *Key* lime pie for a reason. The "Key" part is a vital component. This cookie tastes so much like the pie, from the smooth, limey frosting right down to the graham-crackery, lime-infused cookie.

COOKIES

¾ cup (1½ sticks; 167 g) salted butter, softened

1½ cups (300 g) granulated sugar

1 large egg

1 tsp (5 ml) vanilla extract

2 tbsp (19 g) Key lime zest

1 tbsp (15 ml) freshly squeezed Key lime juice

¼ cup (30 g) sour cream

1½ cups (185 g) all-purpose flour

1 cup (90 g) graham cracker crumbs

½ tsp baking soda

1 tsp (5 g) baking powder

1 tsp (6 g) fine sea salt

GLAZE

3 cups (360 g) confectioners' sugar

2 tbsp (19 g) Key lime zest

2 tbsp (30 ml) freshly squeezed Key lime juice

3 tbsp (45 ml) milk

TOPPING

¼ cup (23 g) crushed graham crackers

Green sugar sprinkles

MAKE THE COOKIES

Preheat the oven to 350°F (180°C) and line 3 baking sheets with parchment paper. Using a stand mixer fitted with the paddle attachment (or a large mixing bowl with a hand mixer), combine the butter, granulated sugar, egg, vanilla, lime zest, lime juice and sour cream and beat on medium speed until creamy and free of lumps.

In a separate bowl, combine the flour, graham cracker crumbs, baking soda, baking powder and salt. Mix well. Gradually add to the butter mixture and beat on medium speed until just combined.

Using a medium cookie scoop, drop the dough by 1½ tablespoons (22.5 g) 2 inches (5 cm) apart onto the prepared baking sheets. Bake in the preheated oven for 9 to 11 minutes, or until golden brown around the bottom edges with no uncooked dough in the centers. Remove from the oven, transfer the cookies to a wire rack and let cool.

MAKE THE GLAZE

Using a stand mixer fitted with the whisk attachment (or a large mixing bowl with a hand mixer), combine the confectioners' sugar, lime zest, lime juice and milk. Beat on medium speed until smooth.

ASSEMBLE THE COOKIES

Drizzle the glaze over the cookies and top with graham cracker crumbs and sprinkles.

NOTE: Before you start juicing these cuties, note that the yellower the Key lime is, the riper (and juicier) it will be!

Triple Chocolate Cake Cookies

MAKES 36 COOKIES

I love chocolate, but I would not consider myself a fanatic. In my opinion, the best piece of chocolate cake is one that I am able to finish. I have never understood the point of paying for a piece of cake if I cannot have more than a few bites. This cookie was created with that idea in mind. It is a miniature version of chocolate cake, but enjoyed without richness overload. This is one of my favorite cookies from this entire collection!

COOKIES

1 cup (2 sticks; 225 g) salted butter, softened

1 cup (225 g) light brown sugar

½ cup (100 g) granulated sugar

2 large eggs

1 tsp (5 ml) vanilla extract

½ cup (120 g) chocolate-nut spread, such as Nutella

2¼ cups (280 g) all-purpose flour

½ cup (55 g) unsweetened cocoa powder

½ tsp baking soda

1½ tsp (7 g) baking powder

1 tsp (6 g) salt

1 (11-oz [310-g]) package milk chocolate chips

FROSTING

½ cup (1 stick; 112 g) salted butter, softened

3 cups (360 g) confectioners' sugar

¼ cup (28 g) unsweetened cocoa powder

2 tsp (10 ml) vanilla extract

3 to 4 tbsp (45 to 60 ml) heavy whipping cream

TOPPING

1 cup (175 g) miniature milk chocolate chips

MAKE THE COOKIES

Preheat the oven to 350°F (180°C) and line 3 baking sheets with parchment paper. Using a stand mixer fitted with the paddle attachment (or a large mixing bowl with a hand mixer), combine the butter, brown and granulated sugar, eggs and vanilla and beat on medium speed until creamy and free of lumps. Add the chocolate spread and beat on low speed until just combined.

In a separate bowl, combine the flour, cocoa powder, baking soda, baking powder and salt. Mix well. Gradually add to the butter mixture and beat on medium speed until just combined. Stir in the chocolate chips.

Using a medium cookie scoop, place 1½-tablespoon-size (22.5-g) chunks of batter in your hands and roll into balls. Place 2 inches (5 cm) apart on the prepared baking sheets and bake in the preheated oven for 10 to 12 minutes, or until the centers of the cookies are cooked through. Remove from the oven, transfer the cookies to a wire rack and let cool.

MAKE THE FROSTING

Using a stand mixer fitted with the whisk attachment (or a large mixing bowl with a hand mixer), combine the butter, confectioners' sugar, cocoa powder and vanilla. Beat on medium speed until moist. Add the cream 1 tablespoon (15 ml) at a time until the desired consistency is reached. Beat on medium-high speed for 3 minutes.

ASSEMBLE THE COOKIES

Spread 2 teaspoons (10 ml) of frosting on each cooled cookie. Top with mini chocolate chips.

Cherry Pie Cookies

MAKES 12 TO 14 COOKIES

This is one of the most-loved and raved about cookies from this entire collection. Simplifying delicious foods is one of my specialties and I feel like I cheated by incorporating the crust into the filling. Plus, cherries are just so vibrant and satisfying. Both of my cookie-loving boys tried nearly every cookie from this book and this is one that comes up in frequent cookie conversation.

CRUMBLE

3 cinnamon-flavored graham crackers, crushed

3 tbsp (42 g) salted butter, melted

COOKIES

2 (9-inch [23-cm]) refrigerated piecrusts

All-purpose flour, for dusting

1 (21-oz [595-g]) can cherry pie filling

1 large egg, beaten

¼ cup (50 g) turbinado sugar, for sprinkling

MAKE THE CRUMBLE

In a medium bowl, combine the graham cracker crumbs and butter. Mix with a fork until the mixture is crumbly. Set aside.

MAKE THE COOKIES

Preheat the oven to 350°F (180°C) and line 2 baking sheets with parchment paper. Roll out the piecrusts onto a flat, lightly floured surface. Using a rolling pin, roll the dough to ⅛-inch (3-mm) thickness. Using a 3-inch (4.5-cm) round cookie cutter, cut circles from the dough. Reroll the remaining dough scraps until all the dough is cut.

Place half of the dough circles 1 inch (2.5 cm) apart on the prepared baking sheets. Top each with 1 tablespoon (15 g) of cherry pie filling, followed by 1 teaspoon (5 g) of the crumble.

Using a sharp knife, cut two ½-inch (1.3-cm) slits into the centers of the remaining dough circles. Place the slit dough circles over the filled dough circles on the baking sheets, pinching the top and bottom circles together at the seams.

Brush the beaten egg over the tops and sprinkle with the turbinado sugar. Bake in the preheated oven for 18 to 22 minutes, or until the cookies are a deep golden brown. Remove from the oven, transfer the cookies to a wire rack and let cool for 5 minutes before serving.

NOTE: Alternatively, you can cut ½-inch (1.3 cm) strips of dough to form a lattice effect. In this case, cut strips from half of 1 piecrust and circles from the remaining 1½ crusts.

Black Forest Cake Cookies

I haven't tasted many bites of Black Forest cake in my life, but the few bites I've had have been memorable. These cookies taste so similar to those delicious bites I've experienced. I tend to think of this combination of flavors as something adults would prefer, but my ten-year-old raves about this cookie.

COOKIES

1 (15.25-oz [432-g]) box devil's food cake mix

2 large eggs

½ cup (120 ml) vegetable oil

½ cup (55 g) sliced almonds

1 cup (175 g) milk chocolate chips

FROSTING

1 (3.5-oz [100-g]) package instant vanilla pudding mix

1 (8-oz [225-g] container) whipped topping, thawed

½ cup (60 g) confectioners' sugar

½ cup (120 ml) milk

1 tsp (5 ml) vanilla extract

TOPPING

1 (21-oz [595-g]) can cherry pie filling

MAKE THE COOKIES

Preheat the oven to 375°F (190°C) and line 2 baking sheets with parchment paper. Using a stand mixer fitted with the paddle attachment (or a large mixing bowl with a hand mixer), combine the cake mix, eggs and vegetable oil and beat on medium speed until creamy. Fold in the almonds and chocolate chips.

Using a medium cookie scoop, drop the dough by 1½ tablespoons (22.5 g) 2 inches (5 cm) apart onto the prepared baking sheets. Bake in the preheated oven for 9 to 11 minutes, or until the centers of the cookies are cooked through. Remove from the oven, transfer the cookies to a wire rack and let cool.

MAKE THE FROSTING

Using a stand mixer fitted with the whisk attachment (or a large mixing bowl with a hand mixer), combine the pudding mix, whipped topping, confectioners' sugar, milk and vanilla. Beat on medium speed for 3 minutes.

ASSEMBLE THE COOKIES

Spread the frosting on the cookies. Top each cookie with 1 to 2 tablespoons (15 to 30 g) of the cherry pie filling.

Mixed Berry Crumble Cake Cookies

MAKES 32 COOKIES

It can be challenging figuring out how to make food look pretty for photographs because not all food is pretty! When berries are involved, food automatically becomes beautiful. I could take pictures of berries all day. My seven-year-old, on the other hand, could eat berries all day. He is my little berry fanatic and when he bit into this cookie, he expressed the utmost pleasure. I love adding berries to crumble cakes in the summer and this cookie is a little snippet of that delicious and beautiful summer treat!

CRUMBLE
½ cup (115 g) light brown sugar

½ cup (60 g) all-purpose flour, plus more as needed

4 tbsp (55 g) salted butter, melted

COOKIES
2 cups (290 g) chopped fresh mixed berries (blackberries, strawberries, blueberries and/or raspberries)

½ cup (100 g) plus 2 tbsp (25 g) granulated sugar, divided

1 cup (2 sticks; 225 g) salted butter, softened

1 cup (225 g) light brown sugar

1 large egg

1 tsp (5 ml) vanilla extract

2 cups (250 g) all-purpose flour

1½ tsp (7 g) baking soda

1 tsp (6 g) salt

1 tsp (2 g) ground cinnamon

MAKE THE CRUMBLE
In a small bowl, combine the brown sugar, ½ cup (60 g) flour and butter. Add extra flour 1 tablespoon (7.5 g) at a time until the mixture is crumbly. Set aside.

MAKE THE COOKIES
In a medium bowl, combine the mixed berries and 2 tablespoons (25 g) of the granulated sugar. Stir and let sit for 10 minutes.

Preheat the oven to 350°F (180°C) and line 3 baking sheets with parchment paper. Using a stand mixer fitted with the paddle attachment (or a large mixing bowl with a hand mixer), combine the butter, brown sugar, remaining ½ cup (100 g) of granulated sugar, the egg and vanilla and beat on medium speed until creamy and free of lumps.

In a separate bowl, combine the flour, baking soda, salt and cinnamon. Mix well. Gradually add to the butter mixture and beat on medium speed until just combined. Fold in half of the fresh mixed berries.

Using a medium cookie scoop, drop the dough by 1½ tablespoons (22.5 g) 2 inches (5 cm) apart onto the prepared baking sheets. Using the back of a spoon, press down slightly into each piece of dough. Place 1 tablespoon (9 g) of the remaining berries on the top of each cookie and sprinkle with the crumble. Bake in the preheated oven for 9 to 11 minutes, or until golden brown around the bottom edges with no uncooked dough in the centers. Remove from the oven, transfer the cookies to a wire rack and let cool.

Lemon Poppy Seed Cake Cookies

MAKES 30 COOKIES

A few years ago, Elijah brought a cute recipe card home from school for Mother's Day that was titled "Mommyseed Cake." I tweaked a few things and over time it turned into a lemon poppy seed cake. It comes out perfectly every time, it is beyond beautiful and it is also simple. Please, I am begging you not to skip out on the lemon curd. It makes these cookies, and in turn you, famous.

LEMON CURD

6 tbsp (84 g) salted butter, softened

1 cup (200 g) granulated sugar

2 large eggs

2 large egg yolks

1 tsp (3 g) lemon zest

⅔ cup (160 ml) freshly squeezed lemon juice

COOKIES

¾ cup (1½ sticks; 167 g) salted butter, softened

4 oz (115 g) cream cheese, softened

1½ cups (300 g) granulated sugar

1 large egg

1 tsp (5 ml) lemon extract, or 1 tbsp (9 g) additional lemon zest

Zest of 1 lemon (about 1 tbsp [9 g])

2 cups (250 g) all-purpose flour

½ tsp baking soda

1½ tsp (7 g) baking powder

1 tsp (6 g) salt

2 tbsp (17 g) poppy seeds

1 cup (120 g) confectioners' sugar

TOPPING

Zest of 1 lemon

MAKE THE LEMON CURD

Using a stand mixer fitted with the paddle attachment (or a large mixing bowl with a hand mixer), combine the butter, granulated sugar, eggs and egg yolks and beat on medium-high speed for 2 minutes. Add the lemon zest and lemon juice and beat until just combined.

Transfer the mixture to a medium saucepan and cook over medium-low heat until smooth. Increase to medium heat and cook, stirring constantly, until the mixture is thick and dark yellow in color, 5 to 7 minutes. Remove from the heat and let cool. Pour into a bowl and cover with plastic wrap; place in the refrigerator.

MAKE THE COOKIES

Preheat the oven to 350°F (180°C) and line 3 baking sheets with parchment paper. Using a stand mixer fitted with the paddle attachment (or a large mixing bowl with a hand mixer), combine the butter, cream cheese, granulated sugar, egg and lemon extract and beat on medium speed until creamy and free of lumps. Add the lemon zest and mix until just combined.

In a separate bowl, combine the flour, baking soda, baking powder, salt and poppy seeds. Mix well. Gradually add to the butter mixture and beat on medium speed until just combined.

Using a medium cookie scoop, place 1½-tablespoon-size (22.5 g) chunks of batter in your hands and roll into balls. Place the confectioners' sugar in a small bowl; roll each ball of dough in the sugar twice, coating completely. Place 1 inch (2.5 cm) apart on the prepared baking sheets. Bake in the preheated oven for 10 to 11 minutes, or until golden brown around the bottom edges with no uncooked dough in the centers. Remove from the oven, transfer the cookies to a wire rack and let cool.

ASSEMBLE THE COOKIES

Top each cookie with 1 tablespoon (15 g) of lemon curd and a pinch of lemon zest.

Red Velvet Cake Cookies

MAKES 46 COOKIES

Do you know how some foods are just so improperly named? Like meat loaf? There are also foods that are perfectly named, such as the delicious red velvet cake. Nothing sounds more satisfying than red velvet. The cookie version of the cake is red and velvety soft in your mouth. This is a great option for gatherings because who doesn't love red velvety treats?

COOKIES

¾ cup (1½ sticks; 167 g) salted butter, softened

1 cup (225 g) light brown sugar

½ cup (100 g) granulated sugar

1 large egg

2 tsp (10 ml) vanilla extract

3 tbsp (45 ml) heavy whipping cream

2 cups (250 g) all-purpose flour

¼ cup (28 g) unsweetened cocoa powder

1½ tsp (7 g) baking soda

½ tsp (2 g) baking powder

1 tsp (6 g) salt

1 (0.25-oz [7-ml]) bottle red food coloring

FROSTING

½ cup (1 stick; 112 g) salted butter, softened

3 cups (360 g) confectioners' sugar

1 tsp (5 ml) vanilla extract

1 tsp (5 ml) almond extract

2 to 4 tbsp (30 to 60 ml) milk

TOPPING

Red sugar sprinkles

MAKE THE COOKIES

Preheat the oven to 350°F (180°C) and line 3 baking sheets with parchment paper. Using a stand mixer fitted with the paddle attachment (or a large mixing bowl with a hand mixer), combine the butter, brown and granulated sugar, egg, vanilla and cream and beat on medium speed until creamy and free of lumps.

In a separate bowl, combine the flour, cocoa powder, baking soda, baking powder and salt. Mix well. Gradually add to the butter mixture and beat on medium speed until just combined. Add the food coloring and mix until the color is spread evenly throughout.

Scoop out tablespoon-size (15-g) chunks of batter and form balls, using your hands. Place 2 inches (5 cm) apart on the prepared baking sheets. Bake in the preheated oven for 9 to 10 minutes, or until the centers of the cookies are cooked through. Remove from the oven, transfer the cookies to a wire rack and let cool.

MAKE THE FROSTING

Using a stand mixer fitted with the whisk attachment (or a large mixing bowl with a hand mixer), combine the butter, confectioners' sugar, vanilla and almond extract. Add the milk 1 tablespoon (15 ml) at a time until the desired consistency is reached. Beat on medium speed for 3 minutes.

ASSEMBLE THE COOKIES

Spread the frosting on the cookies and sprinkle each cookie with sprinkles.

Salted Caramel Apple Pie Cookies

MAKES 28 COOKIES

I dare you to come up with three ingredients off the top of your head that go better together than sea salt, caramel and apples. I fell head over heels in love the first time I tasted this incredible flavor trio. Caramel with a bit of salt sends apple pie somewhere deep into outer space. But let's be real. Apple pie is not the easiest thing to prepare. This cookie tastes even better than the pie, with much greater ease.

FILLING

2 cups (300 g) apple, peeled, cored and chopped in small pieces (about 2 medium apples)

1 tbsp (15 ml) freshly squeezed lemon juice

4 tbsp (55 g) salted butter, melted

½ cup (115 g) light brown sugar

½ cup (100 g) granulated sugar

2 tbsp (14 g) ground cinnamon

COOKIES

1 cup (2 sticks; 225 g) salted butter, softened

1 cup (225 g) light brown sugar

½ cup (100 g) granulated sugar

1 large egg

1 tsp (5 ml) vanilla extract

2 cups (250 g) all-purpose flour

1 tsp (5 g) baking soda

1 tsp (6 g) fine sea salt

1 tsp (2 g) ground cinnamon

TOPPING

1 (12-oz [340-g]) jar caramel ice cream topping, at room temperature

Coarse sea salt

MAKE THE FILLING

In a medium bowl, combine the apples, lemon juice, butter, brown and granulated sugar and cinnamon. Mix well and set aside.

MAKE THE COOKIES

Preheat the oven to 350°F (180°C) and line 3 baking sheets with parchment paper. Using a stand mixer fitted with the paddle attachment (or a large mixing bowl with a hand mixer), combine the butter, brown and granulated sugar, egg and vanilla and beat on medium speed until creamy and free of lumps.

In a separate bowl, combine the flour, baking soda, salt and cinnamon. Mix well. Gradually add to the butter mixture and beat on medium speed until just combined.

Using a medium cookie scoop, place 1½-tablespoon-size (22.5-g) chunks of batter in your hands and roll into balls. Place 2 inches (5 cm) apart on the prepared baking sheets. Press down in the center of each ball, creating a rimmed well.

Scoop 1 teaspoon (5 g) of the filling into the center of each cookie well. Bake in the preheated oven for 10 to 12 minutes, or until the filling is cooked through in the centers. Remove from the oven, transfer the cookies to a wire rack and let cool.

ASSEMBLE THE COOKIES

Drizzle approximately 2 teaspoons (10 g) of caramel over each cooled cookie and sprinkle with sea salt.

Turtle Cake Cookies

"What do turtles have to do with cakes and cookies?" Sammy inquired when I told him the name of this cookie. Good point, but it doesn't matter one bit because *oh my gosh* the combination of pecans, caramel and chocolate is so scrumptious that they could be called Toilet Cookies and I'd still close my eyes and "Mmmmmmm" to the sky. This cookie replicates the irresistible candy absolutely perfectly.

COOKIES
1 (15.25-oz [432-g]) box devil's food cake mix

2 large eggs

½ cup (120 ml) vegetable oil

1 cup (110 g) chopped pecans

1 cup (175 g) semisweet chocolate chips

GLAZE
1 cup (200 g) granulated sugar

½ cup (120 ml) milk

½ cup (1 stick; 112 g) salted butter, cut into pieces

1½ cups (263 g) semisweet chocolate chips

TOPPING
1 (14-oz 400-g]) jar caramel ice cream topping

28 pecan halves

MAKE THE COOKIES
Preheat the oven to 375°F (190°C) and line 3 baking sheets with parchment paper. Using a stand mixer fitted with the paddle attachment (or a large mixing bowl with a hand mixer), combine the cake mix, eggs and vegetable oil and beat on medium speed until creamy and free of lumps. Stir in the pecans and chocolate chips.

Using a medium cookie scoop, drop the dough by 1½ tablespoons (22.5 g) 2 inches (5 cm) apart onto the prepared baking sheets. Bake in the preheated oven for 9 to 10 minutes, or until the centers of the cookies are cooked through. Remove from the oven, transfer the cookies to a wire rack and let cool.

MAKE THE GLAZE
In a medium saucepan, combine the granulated sugar, milk and butter. Cook over medium-high heat, stirring constantly, and remove from the heat immediately after the mixture comes to a boil. Using a whisk, stir in the chocolate chips until the mixture is creamy and free of lumps.

ASSEMBLE THE COOKIES
Dunk the top of each cookie into the chocolate glaze. Top with 2 teaspoons (10 ml) of caramel topping and 1 pecan.

Strawberry Shortcake Cookies

MAKES 30 COOKIES

Every once in a while I come up with a cookie idea that I think will be good and it ends up being more delicious than I ever dreamed. This is that recipe. I love strawberry shortcake. Spongy cake combined with fresh berries and whipped cream, oh my! These cookies are a phenomenal replication of the classic dessert, except taken to another level. My mother-in-law, always very honest with her words, gives these a 10 out of 10.

COOKIES

½ cup (1 stick; 112 g) salted butter, softened

1½ cups (300 g) granuated sugar

1 large egg

2 tsp (10 ml) strawberry extract

½ cup (120 ml) heavy whipping cream

2½ cups (310 g) all-purpose flour

2 tsp (9 g) baking powder

1 tsp (6 g) salt

1 cup (170 g) hulled, chopped strawberries, patted dry

TOPPING

Whipped cream

10 large strawberries, hulled and cut lengthwise into thirds

MAKE THE COOKIES

Preheat the oven to 350°F (180°C) and line 3 baking sheets with parchment paper. Using a stand mixer fitted with the paddle attachment (or a large mixing bowl with a hand mixer), combine the butter, granulated sugar, egg and strawberry extract and beat on medium speed until creamy and free of lumps. Add the cream and mix until creamy and free of lumps.

In a separate bowl, combine the flour, baking powder and salt. Mix well. Gradually add to the butter mixture and beat on medium speed until just combined. Fold in the strawberries.

Scoop 2-tablespoon-size (28-g) chunks of batter in your hands and roll into balls. Place 2 inches (5 cm) apart on the prepared baking sheets. Bake in the preheated oven for 10 to 11 minutes, or until golden brown around the bottom edges with no uncooked dough in the centers. Remove from the oven, transfer the cookies to a wire rack and let cool.

ASSEMBLE THE COOKIES

Top each cooled cookie with 2 tablespoons (30 ml) of whipped cream and a strawberry piece.

Boston Cream Pie Cookies

Boston cream pie contains the most decadent combination of flavors of all time. Yellow cake, creamy vanilla pudding and chocolate? Yes, please! I adore the pie, but I have fallen in love with the cookie version. It's like holding a delicious miniature pie in your fingertips!

COOKIES
1 (15.25-oz [432-g]) box yellow cake mix

2 large eggs

½ cup (120 ml) vegetable oil

FILLING
1 (3.4-oz [100-g]) package instant vanilla pudding mix

1 cup (235 ml) milk

TOPPING
1 cup (175 g) semisweet chocolate chips

½ cup (120 ml) heavy whipping cream

MAKE THE COOKIES
Preheat the oven to 375°F (190°C) and line 2 baking sheets with parchment paper. Using a stand mixer fitted with the paddle attachment (or a large mixing bowl with a hand mixer), combine the cake mix, eggs and vegetable oil and beat on medium speed until creamy and free of lumps.

Using a medium cookie scoop, place 1½-tablespoon-size (22.5-g) chunks of batter in your hands and roll into balls. Place 2 inches (5 cm) apart on the prepared baking sheets and bake in the preheated oven for 8 to 10 minutes, or until golden brown around the bottom edges with no uncooked dough in the centers. Remove from the oven, transfer the cookies to a wire rack and let cool.

MAKE THE FILLING
Using a stand mixer fitted with the whisk attachment (or a large mixing bowl with a hand mixer), combine the pudding mix and milk. Beat on medium speed for 3 minutes.

MAKE THE TOPPING
In a small, microwave-safe bowl, combine the chocolate chips and cream. Microwave on high in 30-second intervals, stirring after each, until smooth and free of lumps. Alternatively, cook the chocolate chips and cream in a medium saucepan over medium-low heat and stir constantly until the mixture is creamy.

ASSEMBLE THE COOKIES
Spread 1 tablespoon (15 ml) of the filling on each cooled cookie. Drizzle with the topping. Refrigerate until ready to serve.

Molten Lava Cake Cookies

MAKES 21 COOKIES

I find an unusual amount of pleasure in hiding food inside other food. I love watching the face of someone who bites into my secret creations. The unexpected nugget of something delicious is so fun and enjoyable. On the outside, a molten lava cake looks like a plain old chocolate cake. When you dig into the center, though, *whoa*. Gooey chocolate gushes out and minds are blown. This cookie is much the same. It appears so simple from the outside, but the centers hold a gooey little soon-to-be-revealed secret. Pull these out of the oven as close to serving time as possible!

¾ cup (1½ sticks; 167 g) salted butter, softened

1 cup (225 g) light brown sugar

1½ cups (300 g) granulated sugar, divided

2 large eggs

1 tsp (5 ml) vanilla extract

2 cups (250 g) all-purpose flour, plus more as needed

½ cup (55 g) unsweetened cocoa powder

1 tsp (5 g) baking soda

½ tsp baking powder

1 tsp (6 g) salt

1 (12-oz [340-g]) jar hot fudge ice cream topping

2 (1-oz [28-g]) squares semisweet chocolate, shaved

NOTE: Start with 2 cups (250 g) of flour and add 2 tablespoons (15 g) at a time if the dough is too soft; the dough will need to be sturdy enough to be handled.

Using a stand mixer fitted with the paddle attachment (or a large mixing bowl with a hand mixer), combine the butter, brown sugar, ½ cup (100 g) of the granulated sugar, eggs and vanilla and beat on medium speed until creamy.

In a separate bowl, combine the flour, cocoa powder, baking soda, baking powder and salt. Mix well. Gradually add to the butter mixture and mix until just combined. Flatten the dough into a disk, wrap in plastic wrap and refrigerate for 2 hours.

Preheat the oven to 350°F (180°C) and line 2 baking sheets with parchment paper.

Remove the chilled dough from the refrigerator. Scoop out 2 tablespoons (30 g) of dough and flatten it into a disk approximately 2½-inches (6.5-cm) in diameter, using your fingers. Place ½ teaspoon of hot fudge topping onto the center and wrap the dough tightly around it, forming a ball. Smooth out the creases in the dough. Repeat the process with the remaining dough and hot fudge topping.

Pour the remaining cup (200 g) of granulated sugar into a small bowl. Roll the dough balls in the sugar, coating completely. Place 2 inches (5 cm) apart on the prepared baking sheets and bake in the preheated oven for 10 to 11 minutes, or until the centers of the cookies are cooked through. Immediately sprinkle shaved chocolate over the tops of the cookies.

Oatmeal Spice Cake Cookies

MAKES 28 COOKIES

My mother-in-law has been making an oatmeal spice cake for years that everyone in the family swoons over. This cookie was inspired by that delicious and satisfying dessert. The cookie is simultaneously crunchy and chewy and you will be tempted to smear the topping over everything in your fridge.

TOPPING

1½ cups (128 g) sweetened coconut flakes

1 tsp (5 ml) vanilla extract

½ cup (120 ml) heavy whipping cream

½ cup (1 stick; 112 g) salted butter, cut into pieces

¾ cup (170 g) light brown sugar

COOKIES

¾ cup (1½ sticks; 167 g) salted butter, softened

1 cup (225 g) light brown sugar

½ cup (100 g) granulated sugar

2 large eggs

1 tsp (5 ml) vanilla extract

1½ cups (185 g) all-purpose flour

1 tsp (5 g) baking soda

½ tsp baking powder

1 tsp (6 g) salt

1 tsp (2 g) ground cinnamon

½ tsp nutmeg

1 cup (80 g) old-fashioned rolled oats

MAKE THE TOPPING

In a medium saucepan, combine the coconut flakes, vanilla, cream, butter and brown sugar. Bring to a boil over medium-high heat. Boil for 1 minute. Remove the pan from the heat and allow to cool completely. Refrigerate until you are ready to assemble the cookies.

MAKE THE COOKIES

Preheat the oven to 350°F (180°C) and line 3 baking sheets with parchment paper. Using a stand mixer fitted with the paddle attachment (or a large mixing bowl with a hand mixer), combine the butter, brown and granulated sugar, eggs and vanilla and beat on medium speed until creamy and free of lumps.

In a separate bowl, combine the flour, baking soda, baking powder, salt, cinnamon and nutmeg. Mix well. Gradually add to the butter mixture and beat on medium speed until just combined. Stir in the oats until combined.

Using a medium cookie scoop, drop the dough by 1½ tablespoons (22.5 g) 3 inches (4.5 cm) apart onto the prepared baking sheets. Bake in the preheated oven for 10 to 11 minutes, or until golden brown around the bottom edges with no uncooked dough in the centers. Remove from the oven, transfer the cookies to a wire rack and let cool.

ASSEMBLE THE COOKIES

Spread the topping on the cookies immediately before serving.

Banana Cream Pie Cookies

MAKES 36 COOKIES

Elijah's friends at school know him as the kid who loves bananas. Every time I ask him what kind of dessert I should make, his reply is, "bananaaaaaaaa . . . something." When I told him I had made cookies that tasted just like banana cream pie, he squealed with excitement. While I think these cookies taste just like the delicious, creamy pie, both of my boys think they taste just like Banana Laffy Taffy. A win either way.

COOKIES

1 cup (2 sticks; 225 g) salted butter, softened

1½ cups (300 g) granulated sugar

2 large eggs

1 tsp (5 ml) vanilla extract

2 cups (250 g) all-purpose flour

1 cup (78 g) crushed vanilla wafer cookies, preferably Nilla Wafers (about 22 cookies)

1 tsp (5 g) baking powder

1 tsp (6 g) salt

FROSTING

1 (5-oz [140-g]) package instant vanilla pudding mix

8 oz (225 g) cream cheese, softened

½ cup (120 ml) milk

TOPPING

1 cup (78 g) chopped vanilla wafer cookies, preferably Nilla Wafers

MAKE THE COOKIES

Preheat the oven to 350°F (180°C) and line 3 baking sheets with parchment paper. Using a stand mixer fitted with the paddle attachment (or a large mixing bowl with a hand mixer), combine the butter, granulated sugar, eggs and vanilla and beat on medium speed until creamy and free of lumps.

In a separate bowl, combine the flour, crushed wafers, baking powder and salt. Mix well. Gradually add to the butter mixture and beat on medium speed until just combined.

Scoop out tablespoon-size (15-g) chunks of batter and form balls, using your hands. Place 2 inches (5 cm) apart on the prepared baking sheets. Bake in the preheated oven for 9 to 11 minutes, or until golden brown around the bottom edges with no uncooked dough in the centers. Remove from the oven, transfer the cookies to a wire rack and let cool.

MAKE THE FROSTING

Using a stand mixer fitted with the whisk attachment (or a large mixing bowl with a hand mixer), combine the pudding mix, cream cheese and milk. Beat on medium speed for 3 minutes.

ASSEMBLE THE COOKIES

Spread 2 teaspoons (10 ml) of frosting on each cooled cookie. Top with the chopped wafers.

Carrot Cake Cookies

My seven-year-old has such an aversion to vegetables that it is comical. The display of drama that accompanies the consumption of any type of veggie is over-the-top ridiculous. When I introduced him to these cookies, he declined them due to the small visible carrot pieces, as I knew he would. When he saw how much the rest of us were enjoying them he reluctantly tried a tiny bite. Of course he loved it because who would ever be able resist something that tastes *just* like carrot cake?

COOKIES

1 cup (2 sticks; 225 g) salted butter, softened

1 cup (225 g) light brown sugar

¾ cup (150 g) granulated sugar

2 large eggs

1 tsp (5 ml) vanilla extract

2½ cups (310 g) all-purpose flour

1 tsp (5 g) baking soda

1 tsp (5 g) baking powder

1 tsp (6 g) salt

1 tsp (2 g) ground cinnamon

¾ cup (110 g) raisins

4 medium carrots, grated (about 2 cups [220 g])

FROSTING

½ cup (1 stick; 112 g) salted butter, softened

8 oz (225 g) cream cheese, softened

3 cups (360 g) confectioners' sugar

2 tsp (10 ml) vanilla extract

MAKE THE COOKIES

Preheat the oven to 350°F (180°C) and line 3 baking sheets with parchment paper. Using a stand mixer fitted with the paddle attachment (or a large mixing bowl with a hand mixer), combine the butter, brown and granulated sugar, eggs and vanilla and beat on medium speed until creamy and free of lumps.

In a separate bowl, combine the flour, baking soda, baking powder, salt and cinnamon. Mix well. Gradually add to the butter mixture and beat on medium speed until just combined. Fold in the raisins and grated carrot.

Using a medium cookie scoop, drop the dough by 1½ tablespoons (22.5 g) 2 inches (5 cm) apart onto the prepared baking sheets. Bake in the preheated oven for 10 to 11 minutes, or until golden brown around the bottom edges with no uncooked dough in the centers. Remove from the oven, transfer the cookies to a wire rack and let cool.

MAKE THE FROSTING

Using a stand mixer fitted with the whisk attachment (or a large mixing bowl with a hand mixer), combine the butter, cream cheese, confectioners' sugar and vanilla. Beat on medium speed for 3 minutes.

ASSEMBLE THE COOKIES

Spread 1 to 2 tablespoons (15 to 30 ml) of frosting on the bottom side of a cookie. Top with another cookie. Repeat the process with the remaining cookies and frosting. Refrigerate until ready to serve.

Sour Cream Raisin Cake Cookies

MAKES 30 COOKIES

I am declaring this cookie to be the most delicious of all of the super simple recipes in this book. Children, adults, food snobs and raisin-haters alike all agree that this is one seriously fantastic cookie. I love that it, just like the cake it is derived from, is insanely easy. The best things usually are!

COOKIES
¾ cup (1½ sticks; 167 g) salted butter, softened

1½ cups (300 g) granulated sugar

1 large egg

1 tsp (5 ml) vanilla extract

½ cup (115 g) sour cream

2 cups (250 g) all-purpose flour

½ tsp baking soda

½ tsp baking powder

1 tsp (2 g) ground nutmeg

1 tsp (6 g) salt

1 cup (145 g) raisins

GLAZE
1 cup (120 g) confectioners' sugar

¼ cup (65 g) sour cream

½ tsp almond extract

MAKE THE COOKIES
Preheat the oven to 350°F (180°C) and line 3 baking sheets with parchment paper. Using a stand mixer fitted with the paddle attachment (or a large mixing bowl with a hand mixer), combine the butter, granulated sugar, egg, vanilla and sour cream and beat on medium speed until creamy and free of lumps.

In a separate bowl, combine the flour, baking soda, baking powder, nutmeg and salt. Mix well. Gradually add to the butter mixture and beat on medium speed until just combined. Fold in the raisins.

Using a medium cookie scoop, drop the dough by 1½ tablespoons (22.5 g) 2 inches (5 cm) apart onto the prepared baking sheets. Bake in the preheated oven for 10 to 11 minutes, or until golden brown around the bottom edges with no uncooked dough in the centers. Remove from the oven, transfer the cookies to a wire rack and let cool.

MAKE THE GLAZE
Using a stand mixer fitted with the whisk attachment (or a large mixing bowl with a hand mixer), combine the confectioners' sugar, sour cream and almond extract. Beat on medium speed until free of lumps.

ASSEMBLE THE COOKIES
Drizzle the glaze over the cookies.

Birthday Cake Cookies

We make a big deal out of birthdays in our house. It's the one day out of the entire year when one person is a star. I keep birthday cakes fairly simple, but I go crazy with cake décor. Sprinkles scream BIRTHDAY HAPPINESS to kids. I notice those little-boy eyes light up when sprinkles adorn baked goods. When *more* sprinkles are used, their eyes light up even more brightly. These cookies are like an eye-brightening birthday cake condensed into a few delicious bites.

COOKIES

1 cup (2 sticks; 225 g) salted butter, softened

1½ cups (300 g) granulated sugar

2 large eggs

2 tsp (10 ml) vanilla extract

2½ cups (310 g) all-purpose flour

1½ tsp (7 g) baking powder

1 tsp (6 g) salt

½ cup (80 g) rainbow sprinkles

FROSTING

½ cup (1 stick; 112 g) salted butter, softened

3 cups (360 g) confectioners' sugar

1 tsp (5 ml) almond extract

1 to 3 tbsp (15 to 45 ml) milk

TOPPING

Rainbow sprinkles

MAKE THE COOKIES

Preheat the oven to 350°F (180°C) and line 3 baking sheets with parchment paper. Using a stand mixer fitted with the paddle attachment (or a large mixing bowl with a hand mixer), combine the butter, granulated sugar, eggs and vanilla and beat on medium speed until creamy and free of lumps.

In a separate bowl, combine the flour, baking powder and salt. Mix well. Gradually add to the butter mixture and beat on medium speed until just combined. Stir in the rainbow sprinkles until just combined.

Scoop out tablespoon-size (15-g) chunks of batter and form balls, using your hands. Place 1½ inches (4 cm) apart on the prepared baking sheets. Bake in the preheated oven for 9 to 11 minutes, or until golden brown around the bottom edges with no uncooked dough in the centers. Remove from the oven, transfer the cookies to a wire rack and let cool.

MAKE THE FROSTING

Using a stand mixer fitted with the whisk attachment (or a large mixing bowl with a hand mixer), combine the butter, confectioners' sugar and almond extract. Add the milk 1 tablespoon (15 ml) at a time until the desired consistency is reached. Beat on medium speed for 3 minutes.

ASSEMBLE THE COOKIES

Spread the frosting on the cooled cookies and top with sprinkles.

Strawberry Cheesecake Cookies

MAKES 30 COOKIES

Sammy loves strawberries almost more than he loves sweets. I knew that combining his two loves would make these cookies a hit, but I didn't anticipate just how much. I had to put them in the way back of the top shelf in our fridge because he would not stop asking, "More, please, Mom? More? Now? Another? When? Now?" Adding strawberries to cheesecakes is one of my favorite ways to enjoy the creamy dessert and I love this cookie, just like my little strawberry-sweets-lover does.

FILLING
8 oz (225 g) cream cheese, softened

½ cup (100 g) granulated sugar

1 large egg

COOKIES
¾ cup (1½ sticks; 167 g) salted butter, softened

½ cup (115 g) light brown sugar

1 cup (200 g) granulated sugar

1 large egg

1 tsp (5 ml) vanilla extract

2 cups (250 g) all-purpose flour

½ tsp baking soda

½ tsp baking powder

1 tsp (6 g) salt

TOPPING
½ cup (198 g) strawberry pie filling

½ cup (60 g) confectioners' sugar

MAKE THE FILLING
Using a stand mixer fitted with the whisk attachment (or a large mixing bowl with a hand mixer), combine the cream cheese, granulated sugar and egg and beat on medium speed for 4 minutes. Using a spatula, scrape the filling into a bowl and place it in the refrigerator.

MAKE THE COOKIES
Preheat the oven to 350°F (180°C) and line 3 baking sheets with parchment paper. Using a stand mixer fitted with the paddle attachment (or a large mixing bowl with a hand mixer), combine the butter, brown and granulated sugar, egg and vanilla and beat on medium speed until creamy and free of lumps.

In a separate bowl, combine the flour, baking soda, baking powder and salt. Mix well. Gradually add to the butter mixture and beat on medium speed until just combined.

Using a medium cookie scoop, place 1½-tablespoon-size (22.5-g) chunks of batter in your hands and roll into balls. Place 2 inches (5 cm) apart on the prepared baking sheets. Press down in the center of each ball, creating a rimmed well.

Remove the filling from the refrigerator. Scoop 1 tablespoon (24 g) of the filling into the center of each cookie well. Bake in the preheated oven for 10 to 12 minutes, or until the filling is cooked in the centers. Remove from the oven, transfer the cookies to a wire rack and let cool.

ASSEMBLE THE COOKIES
Top each cookie with 1 teaspoon (8 g) of strawberry pie filling and dust with confectioners' sugar. Store in the refrigerator until ready to serve.

Rum Cake Cookies

MAKES 40 COOKIES

Just like the cake it is derived from, these cookies are saturated in rum. I absolutely adore a super concentrated rum flavor and these cookies hit the spot. Eating them makes me feel as if I'm breaking the rules in a small and satisfying way.

COOKIES

1 cup (2 sticks; 225 g) salted butter, softened

1½ cups (300 g) granulated sugar

1 (3.9-oz [111-g]) package instant vanilla pudding mix

2 large eggs

1 tsp (5 ml) butter extract

1 tsp (5 ml) rum extract

¼ cup (60 ml) dark rum

3 cups (375 g) all-purpose flour

½ tsp baking soda

1½ tsp (7 g) baking powder

1 tsp (6 g) salt

GLAZE

½ cup (1 stick; 112 g) salted butter, softened

1 cup (200 g) granulated sugar

½ tsp salt

½ cup (120 ml) dark rum

MAKE THE COOKIES

Preheat the oven to 350°F (180°C) and line 3 baking sheets with parchment paper. Using a stand mixer fitted with the paddle attachment (or a large mixing bowl with a hand mixer), combine the butter, granulated sugar, pudding mix, eggs, butter extract, rum extract and rum and beat on medium speed until creamy and free of lumps.

In a separate bowl, combine the flour, baking soda, baking powder and salt. Mix well. Gradually add to the butter mixture and beat on medium speed until just combined.

Using a medium cookie scoop, drop the dough by 1½ tablespoons (22.5 g) 2 inches (5 cm) apart onto the prepared baking sheets. Bake in the preheated oven for 9 to 10 minutes, or until golden brown around the bottom edges with no uncooked dough in the centers. Remove from the oven, transfer the cookies to a wire rack and let cool.

MAKE THE GLAZE

In a medium saucepan, combine the butter, granulated sugar, salt and ¼ cup (60 ml) of water. Cook over medium-high heat, stirring constantly, and remove from the heat immediately after it reaches the boiling point. Stir in the dark rum.

ASSEMBLE THE COOKIES

Drop the cookies, top side down, into the glaze and let sit for 1 minute. Return the cookies to the baking sheets and refrigerate until ready to serve.

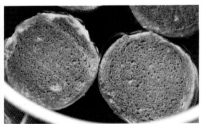

Blueberry Pie Cookies

MAKES 20 COOKIES

Have I mentioned my aversion to making pies? Maybe one day I'll work through this, but I've never been able to understand the painstaking amount of work that goes into a single pie. I'm here to tell you that you can enjoy a pie by transforming it into a cookie! This cookie tastes just like blueberry pie and takes considerably less effort, while also feeding more people (and not totally overstuffing them) than a pie ever would.

COOKIES
2 (9" [23-cm]) refrigerated piecrusts

All-purpose flour, for dusting

1 (21-oz [595-g]) can blueberry pie filling

1 large egg, beaten

GLAZE
2 cups (240 g) confectioners' sugar

¼ cup (60 ml) milk

MAKE THE COOKIES
Preheat the oven to 350°F (180°C) and line 2 baking sheets with parchment paper. Roll out the piecrusts on a flat, lightly floured surface. Using a rolling pin, roll the dough to ⅛-inch (3-mm) thickness. Using a 4-inch (10-cm) round cookie cutter (or the top of a wide-mouth jar or cup), cut circles from the dough. Reroll the remaining dough scraps until all dough is cut.

Place the dough circles 1 inch (2.5 cm) apart on the prepared baking sheets. Top each with 1½ tablespoons (24 g) of the blueberry pie filling. Pull one side of the dough over the filling to create a half circle. Pinch the open edges together at the seams. Using a sharp knife, cut a few slits in the tops.

Brush the beaten egg over the tops. Bake in the preheated oven for 18 to 22 minutes, or until the cookies are a deep golden brown. Remove from the oven, transfer the cookies to a wire rack and let cool for 5 minutes before serving.

MAKE THE GLAZE
Using a stand mixer fitted with the whisk attachment (or a large mixing bowl with a hand mixer), combine the confectioners' sugar and milk. Beat on medium speed until free of lumps.

ASSEMBLE THE COOKIES
Drizzle the glaze over the cooled cookies.

Cinnamon Cream Cheese Crumb Cake Cookies

MAKES 27 COOKIES

In my humble opinion, cream cheese is one of those magical, memorable foods that makes everything taste better. I could add it to any recipe in this book and it would be amazing. My mom used to buy those totally delicious Entenmann's Cheese-Filled Crumb Coffee Cakes when I was a kid and I would sneak into the kitchen and devour forkful after forkful until my stomach couldn't handle another bite. I made this recipe with that irresistible crumb cake in mind. This one is an enormous hit amongst my family members.

FILLING

4 oz (115 g) cream cheese, softened

¼ cup (50 g) granulated sugar

1 large egg

TOPPING

6 tbsp (84 g) salted butter, softened

½ cup (115 g) light brown sugar

½ cup (100 g) granulated sugar

2 tsp (5 g) ground cinnamon

½ cup (60 g) all-purpose flour

COOKIES

1 cup (2 sticks; 225 g) salted butter, softened

1 cup (225 g) light brown sugar

½ cup (100 g) granulated sugar

2 large eggs

2½ cups (310 g) all-purpose flour

1½ tsp (7 g) baking soda

½ tsp baking powder

1 tsp (6 g) salt

2 tsp (5 g) ground cinnamon

MAKE THE FILLING

Using a stand mixer fitted with the whisk attachment (or a large mixing bowl with a hand mixer), combine the cream cheese, granulated sugar and egg. Beat on medium speed for 3 minutes; set aside.

MAKE THE TOPPING

In a medium bowl, combine the butter, brown and granulated sugar, cinnamon and flour. Stir with a fork until crumbly; set aside.

MAKE THE COOKIES

Preheat the oven to 350°F (180°C) and line 3 baking sheets with parchment paper. Using a stand mixer fitted with the paddle attachment (or a large mixing bowl with a hand mixer), combine the butter, brown and granulated sugar and eggs and beat on medium speed until creamy.

In a separate bowl, combine the flour, baking soda, baking powder, salt and cinnamon. Mix well. Gradually add to the butter mixture and mix until just combined.

Using a large cookie scoop, place 3-tablespoon-size (45-g) chunks of batter in your hands and roll into balls. Place 2½ inches (6.5 cm) apart on the prepared baking sheets and press down on each ball slightly with your fingers.

Flour the back of a teaspoon and press it into the center of each dough ball, creating small rimmed wells. Pour the filling into the wells. Sprinkle the topping over the tops. Bake in the preheated oven for 11 to 13 minutes, or until the filling is cooked through in the centers. Remove from the oven, transfer the cookies to a wire rack and let cool.

Cookie Dough Cheesecake Cookies

MAKES 38 COOKIES

I love cheesecake but it's never my first dessert pick. Unless, that is, cookie dough is involved. Cookie dough buried inside the confines of a creamy cheesecake is a ridiculously enjoyable match. Enjoying this delicious marriage in cookie form sends my taste buds into a fit of indulgence. I like keeping the eggless cookie dough portion of this recipe raw, but it can also be baked right into the cookie!

COOKIE DOUGH
½ cup (1 stick; 112 g) salted butter, softened

¾ cup (170 g) light brown sugar

1 tsp (5 ml) vanilla extract

2 tbsp (30 ml) milk

1 cup (125 g) all-purpose flour

½ tsp salt

1 cup (175 g) miniature chocolate chips

COOKIES
½ cup (1 stick; 112 g) salted butter, softened

8 oz (225 g) cream cheese, softened

1½ cups (300 g) granulated sugar

2 large eggs

1 tsp (5 ml) vanilla extract

2¼ cups (280 g) all-purpose flour

1½ tsp (7 g) baking powder

1 tsp (6 g) salt

TOPPING
¼ cup (30 g) confectioners' sugar

MAKE THE COOKIE DOUGH
Using a stand mixer fitted with the paddle attachment (or a large mixing bowl with a hand mixer), combine the butter, brown sugar, vanilla and milk and beat on medium speed until creamy and free of lumps.

In a separate bowl, combine the flour and salt. Mix well. Gradually add to the butter mixture and beat on medium speed until just combined. Stir in the chocolate chips. Wrap the dough in plastic wrap and refrigerate for 1 hour.

Remove the cookie dough from the refrigerator. Using a ¼-teaspoon (1.25-ml) measuring spoon, scoop out chunks of the dough. Roll into balls with your hands.

MAKE THE COOKIES
Preheat the oven to 350°F (180°C) and line 3 baking sheets with parchment paper. Using a stand mixer fitted with the paddle attachment (or a large mixing bowl with a hand mixer), combine the butter, cream cheese, granulated sugar, eggs and vanilla and beat on medium speed until creamy and free of lumps.

In a separate bowl, combine the flour, baking powder and salt. Mix well. Gradually add to the butter mixture and beat on medium speed until just combined. Using a medium cookie scoop, drop the dough by 1½ tablespoons (22.5 g) 2 inches (5 cm) apart onto the prepared baking sheets. Bake in the preheated oven for 10 to 11 minutes, or until golden brown around the bottom edges with no uncooked dough in the centers.

ASSEMBLE THE COOKIES
Immediately press 3 to 4 balls of cookie dough into the top of each cookie. Sprinkle with confectioners' sugar. Refrigerate until ready to serve.

German Chocolate Cake Cookies

MAKES 44 COOKIES

Did you know that German chocolate cake does not come from Germany but is instead named after an American chocolate maker with the last name of "German"? I'm here to clear up this misconception for you because, minus the delicious Black Forest cake, I don't think most people associate Germany with amazingly delicious desserts. You absolutely have to make the cookie version of this cake with the misleading name. The topping is out of this world!

TOPPING

½ cup (1 stick; 112 g) salted butter, softened

1 cup (235 ml) evaporated milk

½ cup (115 g) light brown sugar

½ cup (100 g) granulated sugar

2 large eggs, beaten

1 tsp (5 ml) vanilla extract

1 cup (85 g) sweetened coconut flakes

1 cup (110 g) chopped pecans

COOKIES

1 cup (2 sticks; 225 g) salted butter, softened

1 cup (225 g) light brown sugar

½ cup (100 g) granulated sugar

2 large eggs

1 tsp (5 ml) vanilla extract

2½ cups (310 g) all-purpose flour

½ cup (55 g) unsweetened cocoa powder

1½ tsp (7 g) baking soda

½ tsp baking powder

1 tsp (6 g) salt

½ cup (120 ml) buttermilk

MAKE THE TOPPING

In a medium saucepan, combine the butter, evaporated milk, brown and granulated sugar, eggs and vanilla. Cook over medium heat, stirring frequently, until the mixture is thick, approximately 15 minutes. Remove the pan from the heat and stir in the coconut and pecans. Let cool.

MAKE THE COOKIES

Preheat the oven to 350°F (180°C) and line 3 baking sheets with parchment paper. Using a stand mixer fitted with the paddle attachment (or a large mixing bowl with a hand mixer), combine the butter, brown and granulated sugar, eggs and vanilla and beat on medium speed until creamy and free of lumps.

In a separate bowl, combine the flour, cocoa powder, baking soda, baking powder and salt. Mix well. Gradually add to the butter mixture and beat on medium speed until just combined. Add the buttermilk and mix until combined.

Using a medium cookie scoop, drop the dough by 1½ tablespoons (22.5 g) 2 inches (5 cm) apart onto the prepared baking sheets. Bake in the preheated oven for 10 to 12 minutes, or until the centers of the cookies are cooked through. Remove from the oven, transfer the cookies to a wire rack and let cool.

ASSEMBLE THE COOKIES

Top each cookie with 1 tablespoon (15 ml) of the topping.

Pumpkin Pie Cookies

MAKES 26 COOKIES

I love pumpkin desserts, but at times pumpkin pie can be a bit too intense. It's a concentrated flavor, so eating an entire slice can be too much for me. Enjoying it in its cookie form is the way to go! That yummy pumpkin flavor can be enjoyed without feeling like I'm drowning in it.

FILLING
1 cup (245 g) pure pumpkin puree

⅔ cup (160 ml) evaporated milk

⅔ cup (133 g) granulated sugar

2 large eggs

1 tsp (3 g) pumpkin pie spice

COOKIES
¾ cup (1½ sticks; 167 g) salted butter, softened

1½ cups (300 g) granulated sugar

1 large egg

1 tsp (5 ml) vanilla extract

2 cups (250 g) all-purpose flour

1½ tsp (7 g) baking powder

1 tsp (6 g) salt

TOPPING
Whipped cream

MAKE THE FILLING
Using a stand mixer fitted with the whisk attachment (or a large mixing bowl with a hand mixer), combine the pumpkin, evaporated milk, granulated sugar, eggs and pumpkin pie spice and beat on medium speed for 3 minutes. Set aside.

MAKE THE COOKIES
Preheat the oven to 350°F (180°C) and line 2 baking sheets with parchment paper. Using a stand mixer fitted with the paddle attachment (or a large mixing bowl with a hand mixer), combine the butter, granulated sugar, egg and vanilla and beat on medium speed until creamy and free of lumps.

In a separate bowl, combine the flour, baking powder and salt. Mix well. Gradually add to the butter mixture and beat on medium speed until just combined.

Using a medium cookie scoop, place 1½-tablespoon-size (22.5 g) chunks of batter in your hands and roll into balls. Place 2 inches (5 cm) apart on the prepared baking sheets. Press down in the center of each ball, creating a rimmed well.

Scoop 1½ tablespoons (22.5 g) of the filling into the center of each cookie well. Bake in the preheated oven for 11 to 12 minutes, or until the filling is cooked through in the centers. Remove from the oven, transfer the cookies to a wire rack and let cool.

ASSEMBLE THE COOKIES
Immediately before serving, top each cookie with a squirt of whipped cream.

Triple Chocolate Pecan Pie Cookies

MAKES 36 COOKIES

One Thanksgiving a few years ago, I attempted to make a pie (You did *whaaat?!*). I spent hours putting it together and it looked and smelled delicious. When we arrived at our dinner destination, I set the pie on top of the car so I could grab my boys out of their car seats. As I did so, the glass pie plate slid riiiiight off the top of the car and smashed to smithereens on the pavement below. I was devastated. Glass bits prevented any chance of salvation, so my mother-in-law and I sat on the curb in mourning. This cookie was inspired by that beautiful pie that I'm certain tasted like heaven. I love the chocolate trifecta and the gooey cookie packed with pecans and smelling just like that delicious-smelling dead pie.

COOKIES

¾ cup (1½ sticks; 167 g) salted butter, softened

1 cup (225 g) dark brown sugar

½ cup (100 g) granulated sugar

2 large eggs

1 tsp (5 ml) vanilla extract

2 cups (250 g) all-purpose flour

1 tsp (5 g) baking soda

½ tsp baking powder

1 tsp (6 g) fine sea salt

1 cup (110 g) chopped pecans

1 cup (175 g) dark chocolate chips

1 cup (175 g) semisweet chocolate chips

GLAZE

1 cup (175 g) milk chocolate chips

MAKE THE COOKIES

Preheat the oven to 350°F (180°C) and line 3 baking sheets with parchment paper. Using a stand mixer fitted with the paddle attachment (or a large mixing bowl with a hand mixer), combine the butter, brown and granulated sugar, eggs and vanilla and beat on medium speed until creamy and free of lumps.

In a separate bowl, combine the flour, baking soda, baking powder and salt. Mix well. Gradually add to the butter mixture and beat on medium speed until just combined. Fold in the pecans and chocolate chips.

Using a medium cookie scoop, drop the dough by 1½ tablespoons (22.5 g) 2 inches (5 cm) apart onto the prepared baking sheets. Bake in the preheated oven for 9 to 11 minutes, or until golden brown around the bottom edges with no uncooked dough in the centers. Remove from the oven, transfer the cookies to a wire rack and let cool.

MAKE THE GLAZE

Place the chocolate chips in a medium, microwave-safe bowl. Microwave on high in 30-second intervals, stirring after each, until the mixture is creamy and free of lumps. Alternatively, place the chocolate chips in a small saucepan over medium-low heat and stir constantly until creamy.

ASSEMBLE THE COOKIES

Spread the glaze on the cooled cookies.

Sweet Treats

Cookies inspired by breakfast foods, ice cream and more!

My family's favorites from this section:

Me: Cinnamon French Toast Cookies (page 121)—I love how this cookie has so many similar elements to the breakfast food that inspired it. Not only is the cookie itself beyond delicious, but the frosting is out of this world!

Hubby Dan: Blueberry Buttermilk Pancake Cookies (page 117)—"I was surprised that a pancake could be turned into a cookie and taste so good! I love pancakes and with the cookie version I didn't get messy with syrup but still tasted the syrup flavor."

Elijah (age 10): Neapolitan Ice Cream Cookies (page 118)—"It made me feel like a yummy volcano exploded in my mouth."

Sammy (age 7): Strawberry Sprinkle Donut Cookies (page 122)—"Strawberries are my favorite fruit and donuts are delicious."

I grew up with parents who not only enjoyed sweets, but who allowed me to enjoy all varieties of goodies, as well. I have so many fond childhood memories involving sweets. This is my favorite section of all because I love remembering childhood through tastes, and "sweet treats" encompasses such a wide array of goodies. There are tons of cakes, pies and drinks in the world, but there are even more sugar-laden treats that don't fall into any particular category. Sweet treats include breakfast items, picnic treats, ice cream desserts, candy bars, fudge, pudding, fruity crumbles, ball game fare, sugary finger food and so much more.

I have absolutely loved conjuring up cookies inspired by sweet treats and more than that my boys and I have enjoyed devouring them.

Blueberry Buttermilk Pancake Cookies

When I first sunk my teeth into these babies, I couldn't decide whether I loved the maple frosting or the fluffy blueberry cookies better. So, I ate three more. If ever there was a breakfast that deserved to turn into a cookie, this is it. I shared a few batches of these with various groups of friends and received incredible feedback from all parties.

COOKIES

¾ cup (1½ sticks; 167 g) salted butter, softened

1½ cups (300 g) granulated sugar

2 large eggs

2 tsp (10 ml) vanilla extract

3 cups (375 g) all-purpose flour

½ tsp baking soda

1 tsp (5 g) baking powder

½ tsp salt

½ cup (120 ml) buttermilk

1 pint (340 g) fresh blueberries

FROSTING

2 cups (240 g) confectioners' sugar

½ cup (1 stick; 112 g) salted butter, softened

¾ cup (170 g) dark brown sugar

1 tsp (5 ml) vanilla extract

½ cup (120 ml) real maple syrup

TOPPING

1 pint (340 g) fresh blueberries

MAKE THE COOKIES

Preheat the oven to 350°F (180°C) and line 3 baking sheets with parchment paper. Using a stand mixer fitted with the paddle attachment (or a large mixing bowl with a hand mixer), combine the butter, granulated sugar, eggs and vanilla and beat on medium speed until creamy and free of lumps.

In a separate bowl, combine the flour, baking soda, baking powder and salt. Mix well. Gradually add to the butter mixture and beat on medium speed until just combined. Add the buttermilk and mix until combined. Gently fold in the blueberries.

Using a medium cookie scoop, drop the dough by 1½ tablespoons (22.5 g) 2 inches (5 cm) apart onto the prepared baking sheets. Bake in the preheated oven for 11 to 13 minutes, or until golden brown around the bottom edges with no uncooked dough in the centers. Remove from the oven, transfer the cookies to a wire rack and let cool.

MAKE THE FROSTING

Using a stand mixer fitted with the whisk attachment (or a large mixing bowl with a hand mixer), combine the confectioners' sugar, butter, brown sugar and vanilla and beat on medium speed until creamy. Gradually pour in the maple syrup. Beat on medium speed for 3 minutes.

ASSEMBLE THE COOKIES

Spread 1 tablespoon (15 ml) of frosting on each cooled cookie. Top with the blueberries. Refrigerate until ready to serve.

Neapolitan Ice Cream Cookies

MAKES 32 COOKIES

Did you know that the original colors in Neapolitan ice cream were green, white and red, after the colors in the Italian flag? I'm selfishly thankful for the Americanization of the flavors because vanilla, chocolate and strawberry are like three peas in a pod. This absolutely delicious Neapolitan cookie was born from the same delicious combination of flavors. The wafer cookies hidden inside the cookie batter are the secret stars of the show.

COOKIES

¾ cup (1½ sticks; 167 g) salted butter, softened

1½ cups (300 g) granulated sugar

1 large egg

1 tsp (5 ml) strawberry extract

3 tbsp (45 ml) heavy whipping cream

2 cups (250 g) all-purpose flour

½ tsp baking soda

1½ tsp (7 g) baking powder

1 tsp (6 g) fine sea salt

½ tsp red food coloring

1 cup (115 g) crushed strawberry sugar wafer cookies (about 12 wafers)

FROSTING

½ cup (1 stick; 112 g) salted butter, softened

3 cups (360 g) confectioners' sugar

2 tsp (10 ml) vanilla extract

2 to 4 tbsp (30 to 60 ml) milk

TOPPING

Chocolate syrup or miniature chocolate chips

Colored sprinkles

MAKE THE COOKIES

Preheat the oven to 350°F (180°C) and line 3 baking sheets with parchment paper. Using a stand mixer fitted with the paddle attachment (or a large mixing bowl with a hand mixer), combine the butter, granulated sugar, egg, strawberry extract and cream and beat on medium speed until creamy and free of lumps.

In a separate bowl, combine the flour, baking soda, baking powder and salt. Mix well. Gradually add to the butter mixture and beat on medium speed until just combined. Add the food coloring and mix until the color is spread evenly throughout. Stir in the wafer cookies until combined.

Using a medium cookie scoop, place 1½-tablespoon-size (22.5-g) chunks of batter in your hands and roll into balls. Place 2 inches (5 cm) apart on the prepared baking sheets. Bake in the preheated oven for 10 to 12 minutes, or until golden brown around the bottom edges with no uncooked dough in the centers. Remove from the oven, transfer the cookies to a wire rack and let cool.

MAKE THE FROSTING

Using a stand mixer fitted with the whisk attachment (or a large mixing bowl with a hand mixer), combine the butter, confectioners' sugar and vanilla. Add the milk 1 tablespoon (15 ml) at a time until the desired consistency is reached. Beat on medium speed for 3 minutes.

ASSEMBLE THE COOKIES

Spread the frosting on the cookies and drizzle with chocolate syrup or top with chocolate chips. Top with sprinkles.

Cinnamon French Toast Cookies

MAKES 34 COOKIES

These cookies absolutely blew me away. I took all the delicious ingredients involved in making cinnamon French toast and rolled them up into an irresistible cookie. Then, I topped them with a maple buttercream frosting that made my head spin like the lady from The Exorcist. After eating approximately four of them in a row without breathing, I placed the rest of the batch on our kitchen table and left the house for errands. When I returned, I learned through a pleading note Sammy had written, begging me not to get rid of our dog—Buddy had jumped up on the table and eaten somewhere around ten to twelve of these babies. My first dog endorsement!

COOKIES

1 cup (2 sticks; 225 g) salted butter, softened

1 cup (225 g) light brown sugar

½ cup (100 g) granulated sugar

1 large egg

2 tsp (10 ml) vanilla extract

⅓ cup (80 ml) real maple syrup

3 cups (375 g) all-purpose flour

1½ tsp (7 g) baking soda

1 tsp (6 g) salt

1 tbsp (7 g) ground cinnamon

COATING

2 large eggs, beaten

½ cup (100 g) granulated sugar

3 tbsp (21 g) ground cinnamon

FROSTING

2 cups (240 g) confectioners' sugar

4 tbsp (44 g) salted butter, melted

1 tsp (5 ml) vanilla extract

¼ cup (60 g) real maple syrup

TOPPING

2 tbsp (14 g) ground cinnamon

MAKE THE COOKIES

Preheat the oven to 350°F (180°C) and line 3 baking sheets with parchment paper. Using a stand mixer fitted with the paddle attachment (or a large mixing bowl with a hand mixer), combine the butter, brown and granulated sugar, egg, vanilla and maple syrup and beat on medium speed until creamy and free of lumps.

In a separate bowl, combine the flour, baking soda, salt and cinnamon. Mix well. Gradually add to the butter mixture and beat on medium speed until just combined.

COAT THE COOKIES

Whisk the eggs in a small bowl and mix the sugar and cinnamon together in another small bowl. Using a medium cookie scoop, place 1½-tablespoon-size (22.5-g) chunks of batter in your hands and roll into balls. Roll each ball first in the beaten eggs, followed by the sugar-cinnamon mixture, coating completely.

Place 2 inches (5 cm) apart on the prepared baking sheets and bake in the preheated oven for 10 to 12 minutes, or until the centers of the cookies are cooked through. Remove from the oven, transfer the cookies to a wire rack and let cool.

MAKE THE FROSTING

Using a stand mixer fitted with the whisk attachment (or a large mixing bowl with a hand mixer), combine the confectioners' sugar, butter, vanilla and maple syrup. Beat on medium speed for 3 minutes.

ASSEMBLE THE COOKIES

Spread the frosting on the cookies. Sprinkle with cinnamon.

Strawberry Sprinkle Donut Cookies

MAKES 21 COOKIES

It's funny how crazy kids go over donuts. Add sprinkles and you've hit a total kid jackpot, crazy ringing slot-machine sounds and all. I tease my boys all the time by telling them I'm going to make broccoli donuts covered with frosting and sprinkles. I'm convinced they wouldn't even notice! This particular cookie was inspired by the favorite sprinkled kid treat and it is Sammy's number one most liked cookie from this entire collection. Coming from this sweets fanatic, this is a ringing endorsement!

COOKIES
1 (15.25-oz [595-g]) box strawberry cake mix

1 large egg

½ cup (120 ml) vegetable oil

¼ cup (80 g) strawberry jam

1 tsp (5 g) baking powder

FROSTING
4 cups (480 g) confectioners' sugar

¼ cup (80 g) strawberry jam

¼ cup (60 ml) milk

TOPPING
Colored sprinkles

MAKE THE COOKIES
Preheat the oven to 375°F (190°C) and line 2 baking sheets with parchment paper. Using a stand mixer fitted with the paddle attachment (or a large mixing bowl with a hand mixer), combine the cake mix, egg, vegetable oil, strawberry jam and baking powder and beat on medium speed until creamy.

Using a medium cookie scoop, drop the dough by 1½ tablespoons (22.5 g) 3 inches (4.5 cm) apart onto the prepared baking sheets. Bake in the preheated oven for 8 to 10 minutes, or until the centers of the cookies are cooked through. Remove from the oven, transfer the cookies to a wire rack and let cool.

MAKE THE FROSTING
Using a stand mixer fitted with the whisk attachment (or a large mixing bowl with a hand mixer), combine the confectioners' sugar, strawberry jam and milk and beat on medium speed for 3 minutes.

ASSEMBLE THE COOKIES
Spread 1 tablespoon (15 ml) of frosting on each cooled cookie. Top with sprinkles.

Vanilla Ice Cream Waffle Cone Cookies

MAKES 33 COOKIES

If there were a prize for Most Fun Cookie, this one would win. I love the surprise of discovering a piece of waffle cone buried inside a vanilla-flavored cookie. This cookie wins over an actual ice cream cone because the frosting and sprinkles make it extra fun. I brought a batch into Elijah's fourth grade class and a kid said to me as I was leaving, "Miss Megan? Those cookies were the best things ever." There you go. Nothing beats a kid endorsement like that.

COOKIES

1 cup (2 sticks; 225 g) salted butter, softened

1½ cups (300 g) granulated sugar

1 large egg

2 tsp (10 ml) vanilla extract

2½ cups (310 g) all-purpose flour

1½ tsp (7 g) baking powder

1 tsp (6 g) salt

6 waffle cones, broken into small pieces (about 1½ cups [70 g])

FROSTING

3 cups (360 g) confectioners' sugar

½ cup (1 stick; 112 g) salted butter, softened

½ tsp almond extract

½ tsp vanilla extract

1 to 3 tbsp (15 to 45 ml) milk

TOPPING

Hot fudge ice cream topping, at room temperature

Colored sprinkles

MAKE THE COOKIES

Preheat the oven to 350°F (180°C) and line 3 baking sheets with parchment paper. Using a stand mixer fitted with the paddle attachment (or a large mixing bowl with a hand mixer), combine the butter, granulated sugar, egg and vanilla and beat on medium speed until creamy and free of lumps.

In a separate bowl, combine the flour, baking powder and salt. Mix well. Gradually add to the butter mixture and beat on medium speed until just combined. Stir in the waffle cone pieces until combined.

Using a medium cookie scoop, drop the dough by 1½ tablespoons (22.5 g) 2 inches (5 cm) apart onto the prepared baking sheets. Bake in the preheated oven for 10 to 11 minutes, or until golden brown around the bottom edges with no uncooked dough in the centers. Remove from the oven, transfer the cookies to a wire rack and let cool.

MAKE THE FROSTING

Using a stand mixer fitted with the whisk attachment (or a large mixing bowl with a hand mixer), combine the confectioners' sugar, butter, almond extract and vanilla. Add the milk 1 tablespoon (15 ml) at a time until the desired consistency is reached. Beat on medium speed for 3 minutes.

ASSEMBLE THE COOKIES

Spread the frosting on the cookies. Top with hot fudge topping and sprinkles.

Chocolate Egg Cookies

MAKES 26 COOKIES

When I was a kid, my mom would pack my Easter basket totally full of Cadbury eggs, among other treats. I remember gazing into the sugary centers in awe, wondering how something could possibly be so delicious. When I bite into its cookie counterpart, I have the same thought. These cookies are show-stopping good.

FILLING

½ cup (120 ml) light corn syrup

5 tbsp (70 g) salted butter, softened

2½ cups (300 g) confectioners' sugar

Yellow and red food coloring

COOKIES

¾ cup (1½ sticks; 167 g) salted butter, softened

1 cup (225 g) light brown sugar

½ cup (100 g) granulated sugar

1 large egg

1 tsp (5 ml) vanilla extract

2 cups (250 g) all-purpose flour

½ cup (55 g) unsweetened cocoa powder

1 tsp (5 g) baking soda

½ tsp baking powder

1 tsp (6 g) salt

TOPPING

1½ cups (175 g) milk chocolate chips

MAKE THE FILLING

Place a large piece of waxed paper on a baking sheet and set aside. Using a stand mixer fitted with the whisk attachment, combine the corn syrup, butter and confectioners' sugar and beat on medium speed until creamy and free of lumps. Transfer a quarter of the mixture to a separate bowl and add the food coloring until a deep orange color is achieved. Drop 1 teaspoon (5 ml) of the white filling onto the waxed paper and top it with ¼ teaspoon of the orange filling. Repeat 25 times. Place the baking sheet in the refrigerator.

MAKE THE COOKIES

Preheat the oven to 350°F (180°C) and line 3 baking sheets with parchment paper. Using a stand mixer fitted with the paddle attachment, combine the butter, brown and granulated sugar, egg and vanilla and beat on medium speed until creamy and free of lumps.

In a separate bowl, combine the flour, cocoa powder, baking soda, baking powder and salt. Mix well. Gradually add to the butter mixture and beat on medium speed until just combined. Using a medium cookie scoop, place 1½-tablespoon-size (22.5 g) chunks of batter in your hands and roll into balls. Place 2 inches (5 cm) apart on the prepared baking sheets and press down slightly on each ball of dough. Bake in the preheated oven for 10 to 11 minutes, or until the centers of the cookies are cooked through. Remove from the oven, transfer the cookies to a wire rack and let cool.

MAKE THE TOPPING

Place the chocolate chips in a small, microwave-safe bowl and microwave on high in 30-second intervals, stirring after each, until creamy and free of lumps. Alternatively, place the chocolate chips in a small saucepan over medium-low heat and stir constantly until creamy.

ASSEMBLE THE COOKIES

Top each cookie with a piece of the filling. Drizzle the chocolate over the top.

Frosted Animal Cracker Cookies

MAKES 100 COOKIES

Some things never change and sometimes that is a very good thing. Simply put, when you get something right, don't change a thing. Those delicious pink and white frosted animal crackers with the fun sprinkles look and taste the same as they did when I was a kid. These cookies were created with that fun cracker in mind. I purposely made them small so they would feel more like an indulgent snack, just like the version I remember from childhood.

COOKIES

1 cup (2 sticks; 225 g) salted butter, softened

1 cup (200 g) granulated sugar

1 large egg

1 tsp (5 ml) butter extract

½ tsp almond extract

¼ cup (60 ml) milk

3 cups (375 g) all-purpose flour, plus more for dusting, divided

½ tsp baking powder

½ tsp salt

1 tsp (2 g) ground cinnamon

ICING

2½ cups (300 g) confectioners' sugar

1 tsp (5 ml) almond extract

2 to 5 tbsp (30 to 75 ml) milk

Red food coloring

TOPPING

Round multicolored sprinkles

MAKE THE COOKIES

Using a stand mixer fitted with the paddle attachment (or a large mixing bowl with a hand mixer), combine the butter, granulated sugar, egg, butter extract, almond extract and milk and beat on medium speed until creamy and free of lumps.

In a separate bowl, combine the flour, baking powder, salt and cinnamon. Mix well. Gradually add to the butter mixture and beat on medium speed until just combined.

Place the dough on a large piece of plastic wrap. Wrap the edges around the dough to form a ball and refrigerate for 1 hour.

Preheat the oven to 350°F (180°C) and line 3 baking sheets with parchment paper. Remove the dough from the fridge and sprinkle a flat work surface with flour. Using a rolling pin, roll out the dough to ¼-inch (6 mm) thickness. Use a sharp knife to cut the dough into 1-inch (2.5-cm) squares. Place 1 inch (2.5 cm) apart on the prepared baking sheets and bake in the preheated oven for 7 to 9 minutes, or until the edges are very lightly golden. Remove from the oven, transfer the cookies to a wire rack and let cool.

MAKE THE ICING

Using a stand mixer fitted with the whisk attachment (or a large mixing bowl with a hand mixer), combine the confectioners' sugar and almond extract. Add the milk 1 tablespoon (15 ml) at a time and beat on medium speed until free of lumps.

Transfer half of the icing to a small bowl. Add 1 to 3 drops of red food coloring to the remaining icing and mix on low speed until icing is pink.

ASSEMBLE THE COOKIES

Spread the white icing on half of the cookies and the pink icing on the other half. Top with sprinkles.

Chocolate Raspberry Waffle Cookies

My boys aren't the only kids in the world who get excited about the simple idea of eating breakfast food for dinner. It is fascinating how exciting it is to change the time of day in which you eat a certain type of food. This same thing happened when I turned breakfast food into dessert. Sammy could barely hold himself together, stuttering, "WAFFLES?! . . . Cookies?!" That simple change-up makes these waffle cookies extraordinarily delicious, with a raspberry on top for good measure.

COOKIES

½ cup (1 stick; 112 g) salted butter, softened

1 cup (200 g) granulated sugar

2 large eggs

3 tbsp (60 g) raspberry jam

1½ cups (185 g) all-purpose flour

⅓ cup (37 g) unsweetened cocoa powder

GLAZE

1 cup (200 g) granulated sugar

½ cup (120 ml) milk

½ cup (1 stick; 112 g) salted butter, cut into pieces

1½ cups (263 g) semisweet chocolate chips

TOPPING

26 fresh raspberries

MAKE THE COOKIES

Preheat a waffle maker. Place a large piece of waxed paper on a flat surface. Using a stand mixer fitted with the paddle attachment (or a large mixing bowl with a hand mixer), combine the butter, granulated sugar, eggs and raspberry jam and beat on medium speed until creamy and free of lumps.

In a separate bowl, combine the flour and cocoa powder. Mix well. Add to the butter mixture and beat on medium speed until just combined.

Using a medium cookie scoop, drop the batter by 1½ tablespoons (22.5 g) onto each quadrant of the preheated waffle maker. Close the lid and let cook for 2 to 3 minutes, or until steam stops coming out of the seams. Using a fork, remove the waffle cookies and place on the waxed paper.

MAKE THE GLAZE

In a medium saucepan, combine the granulated sugar, milk and butter. Cook over medium-high heat, stirring constantly, and remove from the heat immediately after it comes to a boil. Using a whisk, stir in the chocolate chips until the mixture is creamy and free of lumps.

ASSEMBLE THE COOKIES

Dunk the tops of the waffle cookies into the glaze and place back on the waxed paper. Top each waffle cookie with 1 raspberry.

Peanut Butter Cup Cookies

MAKES 27 COOKIES

Chocolate and peanut butter is perhaps the most famous flavor marriage of all time. They were absolutely meant to find one another and most of us humans are thankful that they did. My love for Reese's peanut butter cups is shared by many and this re-creation of the popular candy is *spot on*.

FILLING
4 tbsp (55 g) salted butter, softened

1 cup (180 g) creamy peanut butter

½ cup (60 g) confectioners' sugar

2 tbsp (30 ml) milk

COOKIES
¾ cup (1½ sticks; 167 g) salted butter, softened

1 cup (225 g) light brown sugar

½ cup (100 g) granulated sugar

1 large egg

1 tsp (5 ml) vanilla extract

2 cups (250 g) all-purpose flour

½ cup (55 g) unsweetened cocoa powder

1 tsp (5 g) baking soda

½ tsp baking powder

1 tsp (6 g) salt

GLAZE
1 (11-oz [310-g]) package semisweet chocolate chips

MAKE THE FILLING
Using a stand mixer fitted with the whisk attachment (or a large mixing bowl with a hand mixer), combine the butter, peanut butter, confectioners' sugar and milk and beat on medium speed for 2 minutes. Using a spatula, scrape the filling into a bowl and set aside.

MAKE THE COOKIES
Preheat the oven to 350°F (180°C) and line 3 baking sheets with parchment paper. Using a stand mixer fitted with the paddle attachment (or a large mixing bowl with a hand mixer), combine the butter, brown and granulated sugar, egg and vanilla and beat on medium speed until creamy and free of lumps.

In a separate bowl, combine the flour, cocoa powder, baking soda, baking powder and salt. Mix well. Gradually add to the butter mixture and beat on medium speed until just combined.

Using a medium cookie scoop, place 1½-tablespoon-size (22.5-g) chunks of batter in your hands and roll into balls. Place 2 inches (5 cm) apart on the prepared baking sheets. Press down in the center of each ball, creating a rimmed well around the edge.

Scoop 1 tablespoon (10 g) of the filling into the center of each cookie well. Bake in the preheated oven for 10 to 12 minutes, or until the filling is cooked in the center. Remove from the oven, transfer the cookies to a wire rack and let cool.

MAKE THE GLAZE
Place the chocolate chips in a medium, microwave-safe bowl. Microwave on high in 30-second intervals, stirring after each, until the mixture is creamy and free of lumps. Alternatively, place the chocolate chips in a small saucepan over medium-low heat and stir constantly until creamy.

ASSEMBLE THE COOKIES
Spread the glaze on each cooled cookie.

Strawberry Sundae Cookies

MAKES 22 SANDWICHES

More is always better for kids. Without my sound parental advice, my boys would add every possible sugary topping to their ice cream sundaes. Along with age comes the following wisdom: On the topic of sundaes, simpler is better. Nothing beats a purebred strawberry sundae on a hot summer day. These cookies are the perfect transformation of that treat, and I couldn't resist turning them into ice cream sandwiches for an added touch of sincerity.

COOKIES

1 cup (2 sticks; 225 g) salted butter, softened

1 cup (225 g) light brown sugar

½ cup (100 g) granulated sugar

2 large eggs

1 tsp (5 ml) strawberry extract

1 tsp (5 ml) vanilla extract

¼ cup (60 ml) strawberry ice cream topping

½ cup (150 g) chocolate-nut spread, such as Nutella

2½ cups (310 g) all-purpose flour

1 tsp (5 g) baking soda

1 tsp (6 g) salt

1 (12-oz [340-g]) package semisweet chocolate chips

FILLING

1 quart (570 g) vanilla or strawberry ice cream, softened

MAKE THE COOKIES

Preheat the oven to 350°F (180°C) and line 3 baking sheets with parchment paper. Using a stand mixer fitted with the paddle attachment (or a large mixing bowl with a hand mixer), combine the butter, brown and granulated sugar, eggs, strawberry extract, vanilla, strawberry topping and chocolate spread and beat on medium speed until creamy and free of lumps.

In a separate bowl, combine the flour, baking soda and salt. Mix well. Gradually add to the butter mixture and beat on medium speed until just combined. Stir in the chocolate chips.

Using a medium cookie scoop, drop the dough by 1½ tablespoons (22.5 g) 2 inches (5 cm) apart onto the prepared baking sheets. Bake in the preheated oven for 10 to 11 minutes, or until golden brown around the bottom edges with no uncooked dough in the centers. Remove from the oven, transfer the cookies to a wire rack and let cool.

ASSEMBLE THE COOKIES

Sandwich ¼ cup (35 g) of the ice cream between 2 cookies. Repeat the process with the remaining cookies and ice cream. Wrap each sandwich in plastic wrap and freeze for a minimum of 1 hour.

Make your own strawberry ice cream by combining vanilla ice cream and strawberry ice cream topping.

Dark Chocolate Pudding Cookies

MAKES 48 COOKIES

I had a small bowl of dark chocolate pudding recently and just about fell off my chair it was so dreamy and creamy. This cookie was inspired by that bowl of deliciousness that left an imprint on my dessert-loving soul. I made these cookies on a snowy afternoon when my boys had a friend over. I gave each kid a cookie straight from the oven, along with a glass of milk. My boys expressed instant approval, but their friend was silent. I began to wonder if she had qualms when she turned to me and said slowly and deliberately, "These. Are the best. Cookies. I have ever. Eaten. In my life."

1 cup (2 sticks; 225 g) salted butter, softened

1½ cups (340 g) dark brown sugar

1 (3.9-oz [111-g]) package instant chocolate pudding mix

2 large eggs

2 tsp (10 ml) vanilla extract

2 cups (250 g) all-purpose flour

¼ cup (28 g) unsweetened dark cocoa powder

1 tsp (5 g) baking soda

1 tsp (6 g) salt

1 (10-oz [280-g]) package dark chocolate chips

Preheat the oven to 350°F (180°C) and line 3 baking sheets with parchment paper. Using a stand mixer fitted with the paddle attachment (or a large mixing bowl with a hand mixer), combine the butter, brown sugar, pudding mix, eggs and vanilla and beat on medium speed until creamy and free of lumps.

In a separate bowl, combine the flour, cocoa powder, baking soda and salt. Mix well. Gradually add to the butter mixture and beat on medium speed until just combined. Stir in the chocolate chips until just combined.

Scoop out tablespoon-size (15-g) chunks of batter and form balls, using your hands. Place 1 inch (2.5 cm) apart on the prepared baking sheets. Bake in the preheated oven for 9 to 11 minutes, or until the centers of the cookies are cooked through. Remove from the oven, transfer the cookies to a wire rack and let cool.

Oatmeal Cream Pie Cookies

MAKES 50 COOKIES

What snacks come to mind when you think of road trips? Beef jerky? Chips? For me, oatmeal cream pies instantly pop into my head. It's as if they nearly jump off the shelves and hit me in the head when I enter a gas station. That combination of oatmeal cookies and creamy frosting are impossible to resist. Thoughts of marshmallowy frosting danced in my head as I created this to-die-for cookie. I felt ready to hop back in my car and head to the next destination. Mission accomplished.

COOKIES

1 cup (2 sticks; 225 g) salted butter, softened

1 cup (225 g) dark brown sugar

½ cup (100 g) granulated sugar

1 large egg

1 tsp (5 ml) vanilla extract

1½ cups (185 g) all-purpose flour

1 tsp (5 g) baking soda

½ tsp baking powder

1 tsp (6 g) salt

1 tsp (2 g) ground cinnamon

1 tsp (2 g) ground nutmeg

2 cups (160 g) old-fashioned rolled oats

FROSTING

½ cup (1 stick; 112 g) salted butter, softened

1 cup (120 g) confectioners' sugar

1 (7-oz [198-g]) jar marshmallow creme

1 tsp (5 ml) vanilla extract

MAKE THE COOKIES

Preheat the oven to 350°F (180°C) and line 3 baking sheets with parchment paper. Using a stand mixer fitted with the paddle attachment (or a large mixing bowl with a hand mixer), combine the butter, brown and granulated sugar, egg and vanilla and beat on medium speed until creamy and free of lumps.

In a separate bowl, combine the flour, baking soda, baking powder, salt, cinnamon and nutmeg. Mix well. Gradually add to the butter mixture and beat on medium speed until just combined. Stir in the oats until combined.

Scoop out tablespoon-size (15-g) chunks of batter and form balls, using your hands. Place 2 inches (5 cm) apart on the prepared baking sheets. Bake in the preheated oven for 9 to 10 minutes, or until golden brown around the bottom edges with no uncooked dough in the centers. Remove from the oven, transfer the cookies to a wire rack and let cool.

MAKE THE FROSTING

Using a stand mixer fitted with the whisk attachment (or a large mixing bowl with a hand mixer), combine the butter, confectioners' sugar, marshmallow creme and vanilla. Beat on medium speed for 2 minutes.

ASSEMBLE THE COOKIES

Spread the frosting on the cookies and refrigerate until ready to serve.

NOTE: Make your own marshmallow creme by cooking 2 cups (100 g) of mini marshmallows, 2 tablespoons (28 g) of butter and 2 tablespoons (30 ml) of light corn syrup in a medium saucepan over medium-low heat. Cook and stir until free of lumps.

Rocky Road Fudge Cookies

MAKES 50 COOKIES

Rocky road fudge is a morsel of absolute sugary perfection. That's the thing I love about fudge. It is intense and rich, hence the morsel-size servings. I love this treat, as most people do, but I wanted the cookie to feel more like a cookie than fudge but with all of the same incredible flavors. These cookies are thin and crispy and perfectly perfect replications of the famous fudge.

1 cup (2 sticks; 225 g) salted butter, softened

1 cup (225 g) light brown sugar

½ cup (100 g) granulated sugar

2 large eggs

1 tsp (5 ml) vanilla extract

½ cup (150 g) chocolate-nut spread, such as Nutella

2 cups (250 g) all-purpose flour

½ cup (55 g) unsweetened cocoa powder

1 tsp (5 g) baking soda

½ tsp baking powder

1 tsp (6 g) salt

1 (7-oz [198-g]) jar marshmallow creme

1 cup (175 g) semisweet chocolate chips

1 cup (145 g) salted peanuts

1 cup (50 g) miniature marshmallows

Preheat the oven to 350°F (180°C) and line 3 baking sheets with parchment paper. Using a stand mixer fitted with the paddle attachment (or a large mixing bowl with a hand mixer), combine the butter, brown and granulated sugar, eggs, vanilla and chocolate spread and beat on medium speed until creamy and free of lumps.

In a separate bowl, combine the flour, cocoa powder, baking soda, baking powder and salt. Mix well. Gradually add to the butter mixture and beat on medium speed until just combined. Using a wooden spoon, fold in the marshmallow creme, chocolate chips and peanuts.

Using a medium cookie scoop, drop the dough by 1½ tablespoons (22.5 g) 3 inches (4.5 cm) apart onto the prepared baking sheets. Press down slightly on each piece of dough and press 2 or 3 marshmallows into the top. Bake in the preheated oven for 10 to 11 minutes, or until the centers of the cookies are cooked through. Remove from the oven, transfer the cookies to a wire rack and let cool.

NOTE: Make your own marshmallow creme by cooking 2 cups (100 g) of mini marshmallows, 2 tablespoons (28 g) of butter and 2 tablespoons (30 ml) of light corn syrup in a medium saucepan over medium-low heat. Cook and stir until free of lumps.

Jelly-Filled Donut Cookies

MAKES 31 COOKIES

It's amazing how often sweets make me think of my dad. He has the sweetest sweet tooth of anyone I know. Among many other treats, jelly-filled donuts were something he often bought for me as a kid. I clearly remember the excitement of peering into a box of donuts, my tummy preparing with loud growls. This might be where my love for hidden gems inside of food began. I love biting into a donut to discover that a gooey, sugary treat has been waiting for me. These cookies, like the donut, hold a delicious, raspberry-flavored secret.

COOKIES
1 cup (2 sticks; 225 g) salted butter, softened

1½ cups (300 g) granulated sugar

2 large eggs

2 tsp (10 ml) vanilla extract

2½ cups (310 g) all-purpose flour, plus more as needed

2 tsp (9 g) baking powder

1 tsp (6 g) salt

¼ cup (80 g) raspberry jam

GLAZE
2 cups (240 g) confectioners' sugar

¼ cup (60 ml) milk

TOPPING
Colored sprinkles

MAKE THE COOKIES
Preheat the oven to 350°F (180°C) and line 2 baking sheets with parchment paper. Using a stand mixer fitted with the paddle attachment (or a large mixing bowl with a hand mixer), combine the butter, granulated sugar, eggs and vanilla and beat on medium speed until creamy.

In a separate bowl, combine the flour, baking powder and salt. Mix well. Gradually add to the butter mixture and mix until just combined.

Scoop out 2 tablespoons (30 g) of dough and flatten it into a disk approximately 2½ inches (6.5 cm) in diameter, using your fingers. Place ½ teaspoon (3 g) of raspberry jam onto the center and wrap the dough tightly around it, forming a ball. Smooth out the creases in the dough. Repeat the process with the remaining dough and jam.

Place 2 inches (5 cm) apart on the prepared baking sheets and bake in the preheated oven for 11 to 13 minutes, or until the centers of the cookies are cooked through. Remove from the oven, transfer the cookies to a wire rack and let cool.

MAKE THE GLAZE
Using a stand mixer fitted with the whisk attachment (or a large mixing bowl with a hand mixer), combine the confectioners' sugar and milk. Beat on medium speed until free of lumps.

ASSEMBLE THE COOKIES
Dunk the top of each cookie entirely into the glaze twice. Top with sprinkles.

NOTE: Start with 2½ cups (310 g) of flour and add 2 tablespoons (16 g) at a time if the dough is too soft; the dough will need to be sturdy enough to be handled.

Fried Ice Cream Cookies

MAKES 32 COOKIES

My two favorite things about going to a Mexican restaurant are the spicy, cheesy food and the jumbo margaritas. When I was a kid, my favorite thing about Mexican restaurants was the fried ice cream. The flavors from that Mexican dessert are captured perfectly in this cookie. Toss a couple of them into a bowl of vanilla ice cream and close your eyes. Envision a mariachi band standing at your side, for a more true-to-life experience.

1 cup (2 sticks; 225 g) salted butter, softened

½ cup (115 g) light brown sugar

1 cup (200 g) granulated sugar

2 large eggs

1 tsp (5 ml) vanilla extract

2½ cups (310 g) all-purpose flour

1 tsp (5 g) baking soda

½ tsp baking powder

1 tsp (6 g) salt

1 tbsp (2 g) ground cinnamon

2 large egg whites, beaten

2 cups (84 g) crushed sugar-frosted cornflakes

Preheat the oven to 350°F (180°C) and line 3 baking sheets with parchment paper. Using a stand mixer fitted with the paddle attachment (or a large mixing bowl with a hand mixer), combine the butter, brown and granulated sugar, eggs and vanilla and beat on medium speed until creamy and free of lumps.

In a separate bowl, combine the flour, baking soda, baking powder, salt and cinnamon. Mix well. Gradually add to the butter mixture and beat on medium speed until just combined.

Whisk the egg whites in a small bowl and place the crushed cornflakes in another small bowl. Scoop out tablespoon-size (15-g) chunks of batter and form balls, using your hands. Roll each ball first in the beaten egg whites, followed by the cornflakes, coating completely.

Place 2 inches (5 cm) apart on the prepared baking sheets. Bake in the preheated oven for 10 to 12 minutes, or until the centers of the cookies are cooked through. Remove from the oven, transfer the cookies to a wire rack and let cool.

Cannoli Cookies

When I think of cannoli, I'm brought back to watching *The Sopranos* for the first time. Tony Soprano knew good food and the cannoli was no exception. Except, have you ever peeked at a cannoli recipe? Uhh, complicated! The cookie version is far easier and just as delicious, in my opinion. I love the little twist of creamy flavor that the ricotta adds.

COOKIES

1 cup (2 sticks; 225 g) salted butter, softened

1 cup (200 g) granulated sugar

1 large egg

1 tsp (5 ml) vanilla extract

¼ cup (30 g) ricotta cheese

2 cups (250 g) all-purpose flour

½ tsp baking soda

½ tsp baking powder

1 tsp (6 g) salt

1 tsp (2 g) ground cinnamon

1 cup (175 g) miniature semisweet chocolate chips

FROSTING

½ cup (120 ml) heavy whipping cream

1 cup (120 g) confectioners' sugar

1 (15-oz [425-g]) container ricotta cheese

1 tsp (5 ml) vanilla extract

½ tsp ground cinnamon

Zest of 1 lemon (about 1 tbsp [9 g])

TOPPING

1 cup (175 g) miniature semisweet chocolate chips

MAKE THE COOKIES

Preheat the oven to 350°F (180°C) and line 3 baking sheets with parchment paper. Using a stand mixer fitted with the paddle attachment (or a large mixing bowl with a hand mixer), combine the butter, granulated sugar, egg, vanilla and ricotta cheese and beat on medium speed until creamy and free of lumps.

In a separate bowl, combine the flour, baking soda, baking powder, salt and cinnamon. Mix well. Gradually add to the butter mixture and beat on medium speed until just combined. Stir in the chocolate chips until combined.

Using a large cookie scoop, drop the dough by 3-tablespoon-size (45-g) scoops 2 inches (5 cm) apart onto the prepared baking sheets. Bake in the preheated oven for 10 to 12 minutes, or until golden brown around the bottom edges with no uncooked dough in the centers. Remove from the oven, transfer the cookies to a wire rack and let cool.

MAKE THE FROSTING

Using a stand mixer fitted with the whisk attachment (or a large mixing bowl with a hand mixer), beat the cream on high speed until stiff peaks form (3 to 5 minutes). Using a spatula, scrape into a small bowl and set aside.

In the same mixer bowl, combine the confectioners' sugar, ricotta cheese, vanilla and cinnamon. Beat on high speed for 3 minutes. Add the lemon zest and mix until just combined. Fold in the reserved cream.

ASSEMBLE THE COOKIES

Spread the frosting on the cookies and top with chocolate chips. Refrigerate until ready to serve.

Chocolate Peanut Cookies

MAKES 34 COOKIES

I had a serious love for candy bars as a kid. Almost every night before bed my dad, who shares my love for *everything* sweet, would make an ice cream concoction for us to share. It usually involved vanilla ice cream along with whichever type of candy bar was in the house. I was extra giddy whenever Snickers were involved because those creations could not be beat. These cookies taste just like that delicious candy bar that I've longed for so many times. The marshmallow creme in the recipe is the secret star of the show!

COOKIES

¾ cup (1½ sticks; 167 g) salted butter, softened

1 cup (200 g) granulated sugar

1 large egg

1 tsp (5 ml) vanilla extract

¼ cup (65 g) creamy peanut butter

2¼ cups (280 g) all-purpose flour

½ tsp baking soda

½ tsp baking powder

1 tsp (6 g) salt

1 (7-oz [198-g]) jar marshmallow creme (see note on page 141)

1 cup (154 g) caramel bits

¾ cup (109 g) salted peanuts

TOPPING

1½ cups (263 g) milk chocolate chips

¼ cup (65 g) creamy peanut butter

MAKE THE COOKIES

Preheat the oven to 350°F (180°C) and line 3 baking sheets with parchment paper. Using a stand mixer fitted with the paddle attachment (or a large mixing bowl with a hand mixer), combine the butter, granulated sugar, egg and vanilla and beat on medium speed until creamy. Add the peanut butter and beat on low speed until just combined.

In a separate bowl, combine the flour, baking soda, baking powder and salt. Mix well. Gradually add to the butter mixture and beat on medium speed until just combined. Using a wooden spoon, fold in the marshmallow creme, caramel bits and peanuts.

Using a medium cookie scoop, place 1½-tablespoon-size (22.5-g) chunks of batter in your hands and roll into balls. Place 2 inches (5 cm) apart on the prepared baking sheets and bake in the preheated oven for 11 to 13 minutes, or until golden brown around the bottom edges with no uncooked dough in the centers. Remove from the oven, transfer the cookies to a wire rack and let cool.

MAKE THE TOPPING

In a small, microwave-safe bowl, combine the chocolate chips and peanut butter. Microwave on high in 30-second intervals, stirring after each, until smooth and free of lumps. Alternatively, combine the chocolate chips and peanut butter in a medium saucepan over medium-low heat and stir constantly until the mixture is creamy.

ASSEMBLE THE COOKIES

Spread 1 tablespoon (15 ml) of the topping on each cookie and spread with the back of a spoon to cover the surface. Refrigerate until ready to serve.

Cinnamon Roll Cookies

MAKES 28 COOKIES

I don't think I need to tell you how time-consuming and tedious cinnamon rolls are to make. Despite my negative notions about the process involved in making them, they are one of the tastiest creations ever in the history of life. The good news is that turning them into a cookie requires far less work and they come out tasting just like the gooey, sugary breakfast treat.

FILLING

3 tbsp (42 g) unsalted butter, melted

½ cup (115 g) light brown sugar

1 tbsp (7 g) ground cinnamon

COOKIES

1 cup (2 sticks; 225 g) salted butter, softened

1 cup (200 g) granulated sugar

1 large egg

1 tsp (5 ml) vanilla extract

2 cups (250 g) all-purpose flour

½ tsp baking powder

1 tsp (6 g) salt

ICING

2 cups (240 g) confectioners' sugar

1 tsp (5 ml) vanilla extract

¼ cup (60 ml) milk

NOTE: When rolling the dough into a log, loosen from your work surface with a spatula if sticking occurs. If cracks form as you roll, smooth them out with your fingers as you go.

MAKE THE FILLING

In a small bowl, combine the butter, brown sugar and cinnamon. Mix well and set aside.

MAKE THE COOKIES

Using a stand mixer fitted with the paddle attachment (or a large mixing bowl with a hand mixer), combine the butter, granulated sugar, egg and vanilla and beat on medium speed until creamy and free of lumps.

In a separate bowl, combine the flour, baking powder and salt. Mix well. Gradually add to the butter mixture and beat on medium speed until just combined.

Generously sprinkle a flat work surface with flour. Using a rolling pin, roll out the dough to a large rectangle ½ inch (1.3 cm) thick. Use a sharp knife to cut straight sides, forming a 10 x 14-inch (25.5 x 34.5-cm) rectangle. Spread an even layer of the filling on the dough, leaving a 1-inch (2.5-cm) margin along all the edges. Starting with a long edge, roll the dough into a log. Wrap the log in plastic wrap and refrigerate for 2 hours.

Preheat the oven to 350°F (180°C) and line 3 baking sheets with parchment paper. Remove the log from the refrigerator and, using a sharp knife, cut off ½-inch (1.3-cm) slices. Place 1 inch (2.5 cm) apart on the prepared baking sheets and bake in the preheated oven for 11 to 12 minutes, or until the edges are very lightly golden. Remove from the oven, transfer the cookies to a wire rack and let cool.

MAKE THE ICING

Using a stand mixer fitted with the whisk attachment (or a large mixing bowl with a hand mixer), combine the confectioners' sugar and vanilla. Add the milk 1 tablespoon (15 ml) at a time and beat on medium speed until free of lumps.

ASSEMBLE THE COOKIES

Generously drizzle the icing on the cookies.

Triple Chocolate Fudge Cookies

MAKES 40 COOKIES

I love how in dessert speak, "triple chocolate" doesn't just mean three times the chocolate. It means three *different types* of chocolate all in the same place. There are so many incredible chocolate varieties in our world of endless options. If you bite into a piece of fudge knowing there are three different chocolates involved, it instantly becomes more enjoyable and decadent. Each type of chocolate offers something a little bit different, which makes the fudge *and* this cookie fashioned after it so well-rounded and gratifying.

1 cup (2 sticks; 225 g) salted butter, softened

1 cup (225 g) light brown sugar

1 cup (200 g) granulated sugar

2 large eggs

2 tsp (10 ml) vanilla extract

2 cups (250 g) all-purpose flour

½ cup (55 g) unsweetened cocoa powder

1½ tsp (7 g) baking soda

1 tsp (6 g) salt

1 cup (175 g) dark chocolate chips

1 cup (175 g) semisweet chocolate chips

Preheat the oven to 350°F (180°C) and line 3 baking sheets with parchment paper. Using a stand mixer fitted with the paddle attachment (or a large mixing bowl with a hand mixer), combine the butter, brown and granulated sugar, eggs and vanilla and beat on medium speed until creamy and free of lumps.

In a separate bowl, combine the flour, cocoa powder, baking soda and salt. Mix well. Gradually add to the butter mixture and beat on medium speed until just combined. Stir in the chocolate chips.

Using a medium cookie scoop, drop the dough by 1½ tablespoons (22.5 g) 2 inches (5 cm) apart onto the prepared baking sheets. Bake in the preheated oven for 9 to 11 minutes, or until the centers of the cookies are cooked through. Remove from the oven, transfer the cookies to a wire rack and let cool.

Chocolate Almond Cookies

MAKES 32 COOKIES

Almond Joy candy bars are among the most underrated candies on the planet. I find extra pleasure in enjoying underrated things because I love feeling like I'm keeping a fun little secret from the rest of the world. Transforming this coconutty, chocolaty treat into a cookie is insanely satisfying!

¾ cup (1½ sticks; 167 g) salted butter, softened

1 cup (225 g) light brown sugar

½ cup (100 g) granulated sugar

2 large eggs

1 tsp (5 ml) coconut extract

2 cups (250 g) all-purpose flour

1 tsp (5 g) baking soda

1 tsp (6 g) salt

¾ cup (64 g) sweetened shredded coconut

1 cup (175 g) semisweet chocolate chunks

½ cup (55 g) chopped almonds

Preheat the oven to 350°F (180°C) and line 3 baking sheets with parchment paper. Using a stand mixer fitted with the paddle attachment (or a large mixing bowl with a hand mixer), combine the butter, brown and granulated sugar, eggs and coconut extract and beat on medium speed until creamy and free of lumps.

In a separate bowl, combine the flour, baking soda and salt. Mix well. Gradually add to the butter mixture and beat on medium speed until just combined. Stir in the coconut, chocolate chunks and almonds.

Using a medium cookie scoop, place 1½-tablespoon-size (22.5-g) chunks of batter in your hands and roll into balls. Place 2 inches (5 cm) apart on the prepared baking sheets and bake in the preheated oven for 10 to 11 minutes, or until golden brown around the bottom edges with no uncooked dough in the centers. Remove from the oven, transfer the cookies to a wire rack and let cool.

Banana Split Cookies

Banana splits stress me out. There's so much to eat! What if I miss out on something? What if I get too full or the ice cream melts into a gooey puddle? Ice cream has a short life span, people! I was a bit more excited to make this cookie than most others because it was an opportunity to condense a bunch of totally irresistible flavors into one bite. You'll have to open wide to squeeze it all in, but you won't miss out on a thing! For a bonus, crumble a few and throw them into a bowl of vanilla ice cream.

COOKIES

¾ cup (1½ sticks; 167 g) salted butter, softened

1 cup (225 g) light brown sugar

½ cup (100 g) granulated sugar

1 large egg

1 tsp (5 ml) vanilla extract

2¼ cups (280 g) all-purpose flour

1½ tsp (7 g) baking soda

½ cup (55 g) unsweetened cocoa powder

1 tsp (6 g) salt

1 ripe banana, mashed

1 cup (170 g) hulled, chopped strawberries, patted dry

1 cup (175 g) semisweet chocolate chips

TOPPING

Caramel ice cream topping, at room temperature

Whipped cream

30 maraschino cherries

MAKE THE COOKIES

Preheat the oven to 350°F (180°C) and line 3 baking sheets with parchment paper. Using a stand mixer fitted with the paddle attachment (or a large mixing bowl with a hand mixer), combine the butter, brown and granulated sugar, egg and vanilla and beat on medium speed until creamy and free of lumps.

In a separate bowl, combine the flour, baking soda, cocoa powder and salt. Mix well. Gradually add to the butter mixture and beat on medium speed until just combined. Stir in the banana, strawberries and chocolate chips.

Using a medium cookie scoop, drop the dough by 1½ tablespoons (22.5 g) 2 inches (5 cm) apart onto the prepared baking sheets. Bake in the preheated oven for 10 to 11 minutes, or until the centers of the cookies are cooked through. Remove from the oven, transfer the cookies to a wire rack and let cool.

ASSEMBLE THE COOKIES

Immediately before serving, top each cookie with 1 tablespoon (15 ml) of caramel topping, a squirt of whipped cream and 1 cherry.

Chocolate Peanut Butter Crispy Rice Cookies

As if Rice Krispies treats weren't delicious enough, someone had to go and add not only chocolate to the mix but peanut butter, too? This is one of my all-time favorite easy desserts, along with every other human who can swallow food. When a friend bit into this cookie that was inspired by the classic treat, it was followed by an "I love you."

1 cup (2 sticks; 225 g) salted butter, softened

1½ cups (300 g) granulated sugar

2 large eggs

1 tsp (5 ml) vanilla extract

½ cup (130 g) creamy peanut butter

2 cups (250 g) all-purpose flour

½ tsp baking soda

1 tsp (2 g) baking powder

1 tsp (6 g) salt

1 (7-oz [198-g]) jar marshmallow creme

1 cup (175 g) semisweet chocolate chips

2 cups (42 g) crispy rice cereal, such as Rice Krispies

Preheat the oven to 350°F (180°C) and line 3 baking sheets with parchment paper. Using a stand mixer fitted with the paddle attachment (or a large mixing bowl with a hand mixer), combine the butter, granulated sugar, eggs, vanilla and peanut butter and beat on medium speed until creamy and free of lumps.

In a separate bowl, combine the flour, baking soda, baking powder and salt. Mix well. Gradually add to the butter mixture and beat on medium speed until just combined. Using a wooden spoon, stir in the marshmallow creme, chocolate chips and cereal until combined.

Using a medium cookie scoop, drop the dough by 1½ tablespoons (22.5 g) 2 inches (5 cm) apart onto the prepared baking sheets. Bake in the preheated oven for 8 to 10 minutes, or until golden brown around the bottom edges with no uncooked dough in the centers. Remove from the oven, transfer the cookies to a wire rack and let cool.

NOTE: Make your own marshmallow creme by cooking 2 cups (100 g) of mini marshmallows, 2 tablespoons (28 g) of butter and 2 tablespoons (30 ml) of light corn syrup in a medium saucepan over medium-low heat. Cook and stir until free of lumps.

Creamy Orange Cookies

MAKES 22 COOKIES

Orange is by far my favorite flavor of the iconic American ice cream-filled Creamsicle. The frozen orange-vanilla combo is a dreamy one. This cookie reminds me of the childhood indulgence that put a smile on my face time and time again when I was a kid.

COOKIES

½ cup (1 stick; 112 g) salted butter, softened

1½ cups (300 g) granulated sugar

½ cup (60 g) sour cream

½ cup (120 ml) heavy whipping cream

½ tsp orange extract, or 3 tbsp (45 ml) freshly squeezed orange juice

Zest of 1 orange (about 1 tbsp [9 g])

2½ cups (250 g) all-purpose flour

1 tsp (5 g) baking soda

1 tsp (5 g) baking powder

1 cup (175 g) white chocolate chips

TOPPING

Orange zest and/or orange sugar sprinkles

MAKE THE COOKIES

Preheat the oven to 350°F (180°C) and line 3 baking sheets with parchment paper. Using a stand mixer fitted with the paddle attachment (or a large mixing bowl with a hand mixer), combine the butter, granulated sugar, sour cream, cream and orange extract and beat on medium speed until creamy and free of lumps. Add the orange zest and mix until just combined.

In a separate bowl, combine the flour, baking soda and baking powder. Mix well. Gradually add to the butter mixture and beat on medium speed until just combined. Stir in the white chocolate chips.

Using a medium cookie scoop, drop the dough by 1½ tablespoons (22.5 g) 2 inches (5 cm) apart onto the prepared baking sheets. Bake in the preheated oven for 10 to 11 minutes, or until golden brown around the bottom edges with no uncooked dough in the centers. Remove from the oven, transfer the cookies to a wire rack and let cool.

ASSEMBLE THE COOKIES

Sprinkle orange zest and/or sprinkles over the cookies.

S'mores Cookies

Both of my boys are totally addicted to s'mores. I'm talking, possible intervention may be required. We spent six weeks traveling the western United States in our RV last summer and in my boys' eyes, every campground we stopped at was an opportunity to make and devour s'mores. I don't think there is a better summertime treat than this one. Ooey-gooey, slightly-charred marshmallows topped with melted chocolate and sandwiched between sugary graham crackers? This almost beats out the peanut butter–chocolate marriage. I meant for this insanely irresistible cookie version to be slightly crispy, just like its campfire pioneer.

1 cup (2 sticks; 225 g) salted butter, softened

½ cup (115 g) light brown sugar

1 cup (200 g) granulated sugar

2 large eggs

2 tsp (10 ml) vanilla extract

1½ cups (185 g) all-purpose flour

1¼ cups (113 g) graham cracker crumbs (8 crackers)

½ tsp baking soda

1 tsp (5 g) baking powder

1 tsp (6 g) salt

1 (12-oz [340-g]) package semisweet chocolate chips

4 (1.55-oz [44-g]) milk chocolate candy bars, such as Hershey's, coarsely chopped

1 cup (50 g) miniature marshmallows

7 graham crackers, broken into pieces

Preheat the oven to 350°F (180°C) and line 3 baking sheets with parchment paper. Using a stand mixer fitted with the paddle attachment (or a large mixing bowl with a hand mixer), combine the butter, brown and granulated sugar, eggs and vanilla and beat on medium speed until creamy and free of lumps.

In a separate bowl, combine the flour, graham cracker crumbs, baking soda, baking powder and salt. Mix well. Gradually add to the butter mixture and beat on medium speed until just combined. Stir in the chocolate chips until combined.

Using a medium cookie scoop, drop the dough by 1½ tablespoons (22.5 g) 2 inches (5 cm) apart onto the prepared baking sheets. Bake in the preheated oven for 9 minutes. Immediately top the cookies with the chocolate pieces, marshmallows and graham cracker pieces. Place back in the oven and bake for an additional 2 minutes. Remove from the oven, transfer the cookies to a wire rack and let cool.

Pecan Candy Cookies

MAKES 33 COOKIES

I love the history behind Turtles candies. First of all, the pecan-chocolate-caramel candy has been around for almost 100 years. Longevity like that speaks volumes. Someone touring the candy-making facility in the early 1900s pointed out that after the candy had been dipped in chocolate, it resembled a turtle. Soon after, the candy was sold under the name "Turtles." Resembling and being named after a cute sea creature makes the candy somehow more delicious. I made these cookies with those candies in mind and personally think it's one of the better impersonations from the entire collection.

COOKIES

¾ cup (1½ sticks; 167 g) salted butter, softened

1 cup (225 g) light brown sugar

⅓ cup (67 g) granulated sugar

1 large egg

1 tsp (5 ml) vanilla extract

2¼ cups (280 g) all-purpose flour

1 tsp (5 g) baking soda

½ tsp baking powder

1 tsp (6 g) salt

1 (11-oz [310 g]) package caramel bits

1 cup (110 g) chopped pecans

GLAZE

1 (11-oz [310-g]) package semisweet chocolate chips

TOPPING

33 pecan halves

MAKE THE COOKIES

Preheat the oven to 350°F (180°C) and line 3 baking sheets with parchment paper. Using a stand mixer fitted with the paddle attachment (or a large mixing bowl with a hand mixer), combine the butter, brown and granulated sugar, egg and vanilla and beat on medium speed until creamy and free of lumps.

In a separate bowl, combine the flour, baking soda, baking powder and salt. Mix well. Gradually add to the butter mixture and beat on medium speed until just combined. Fold in the caramel bits and pecans.

Using a medium cookie scoop, place 1½-tablespoon-size (22.5-g) chunks of batter in your hands and roll into balls. Place 2 inches (5 cm) apart on the prepared baking sheets and bake in the preheated oven for 10 to 11 minutes, or until golden brown around the bottom edges with no uncooked dough in the centers. Remove from the oven, transfer the cookies to a wire rack and let cool.

MAKE THE GLAZE

Place the chocolate chips in a medium, microwave-safe bowl. Microwave on high in 30-second intervals, stirring after each, until the mixture is creamy and free of lumps. Alternatively, place the chocolate chips in a small saucepan over medium-low heat and stir constantly until creamy.

ASSEMBLE THE COOKIES

Drizzle the chocolate over the cookies and top each with a pecan half.

Resources

I created the recipes in this book with the beginner baker in mind.

It's true what people say—baking *is* a science. However, it should not be scary and it is way too fun and delicious to be avoided. Not all baking mistakes need to be dumped in the garbage and you can make an amazing recipe with easy-to-find ingredients and very few pieces of equipment. I have learned that I am my most critical critic and that the majority of people don't even notice minor baking mistakes.

Equipment

Keeping things simple in the kitchen is a necessity for me. When I open a cookbook, I like to know that I will be able to make everything in the book with the tools already in my kitchen, with few and affordable exceptions. Read through the equipment list that follows and decide what you have and what you want to run out and get. At bare minimum, you can make every single recipe in this entire book by using the following: one baking sheet, basic measuring cups and spoons, a mixing spoon, a stand or hand mixer and a grater. Anything extra is icing on the cake, er, cookie!

My personal cookie-making equipment:

BAKING SHEETS

Aluminum baking pans or cookie sheets are affordable and they uniformly conduct heat, making them an excellent choice for baking cookies. I bake all of my cookies on a heavy-duty aluminum half sheet pan. These measure at 13 x 18 inches (33 x 45.5 cm), which can fit into standard-size ovens and one pan easily has enough room for fifteen regular-size cookies. Other smaller aluminum baking sheets will provide other benefits, such as rimless edges for easy pan-to-wire-cooling-rack cookie transfer. Any aluminum pan is a great option for cookies, but whichever kind you choose, I highly recommend lining baking sheets with parchment paper or a silicone mat.

PARCHMENT PAPER/SILICONE MATS

Baking with the magical parchment paper is a personal must, for the following reasons:

- It resists both grease and moisture.

- Baked goods will not stick to it.

- Aluminum pans can react to acidic ingredients, creating a metallic taste; parchment paper will eliminate this issue.

- It makes cleanup an absolutely wonderful, no-pan-scrubbing experience. I'm talking, throw that thing right back into the cupboard.

- The paper can be reused several times, until it begins to look crispy or brittle as if pleading with you to end its life.

If you find that you are going through a ton of parchment paper, silicone mats are a great replacement. They will save money if you bake a lot and they also give a nod to the environment. They are nonstick baking mats that are easy to clean and store.

MEASURING CUPS AND SPOONS
Standard US 1-cup, ½-cup, ⅓-cup and ¼-cup measuring cups are used throughout the book, as well as 1-tablespoon and 1-, ½- and ¼-teaspoon measuring spoons. A 2-cup liquid measuring cup is handy for the recipes containing liquid ingredients, but not a necessity. Every measurement is followed by its metric equivalent (volume for pourable liquids, weight for solid ingredients).

COOKIE SCOOPS/COOKIE CUTTERS
Most of the cookies in this book were made using a medium (1½-tablespoon [22.5-g]) cookie scoop. I have secretly fallen in love with this cookie scoop for the following reasons:

- 1½ tablespoons (22.5 g) of dough is the perfect size for most cookies.

- It makes dropping dough onto baking sheets super easy and quick.

- It creates cookies that are the same size and shape.

- No cooking spray is required and the batter will not stick to the insides.

- It can be used for ice cream, fruit, meatballs, cupcakes and more!

Despite my love for the medium scoop, getting by without one is doable. Use a large spoon or a 1-tablespoon (15-g) measuring spoon and load it up with a heaping scoop of batter. Use your fingers to drop the batter onto the baking sheet.

A large (3-tablespoon [45-g]) cookie scoop is used only a handful of times in this book and is definitely not worth purchasing. If you own one, great! If not, scoop out 3 tablespoons (45 g) of the cookie batter and form it into one big ball with your hands.

I used a 1-tablespoon (15-g) measuring spoon to measure dough for cookies I thought should be on the smaller side and also that could easily be handled and rolled into balls.

There are a few shortbread cookies in the book that require round cookie cutters. The sizes in diameter needed are: 1½, 2½, 3 and 4 inches (4, 6.5, 7.5 and 10 cm). Look around your kitchen and I'll bet you can cover all of these sizes with rims of glasses and jars.

STAND MIXER/HAND MIXER

It doesn't matter which you use, because both will yield great results, but you will need either a stand or a hand mixer for every cookie in this book. With the stand mixer, you'll need both paddle and whisk attachments and you'll be able to walk away to complete other tasks while the batter or frosting is mixing. With the hand mixer, you'll use the standard beater attachments for all mixing and you won't have the option of leaving the bowl's side. Watch out for those beaters, though. I hear people get their fingers caught in them, resulting in months of agony and hand therapy.

COFFEE GRINDER/SMALL FOOD PROCESSOR

A few recipes require grinding freeze-dried fruit into a powder. A coffee grinder or small food processor will get the job done for you in a matter of seconds. If you do not own either of these, borrow one from a neighbor. If your neighbor is out of town, place the fruit pieces in a resealable plastic bag and grab a large, heavy wooden spoon. Think of someone who causes stress in your life and pound away at the fruit until you have pulverized it to bits. It is my pleasure to provide tips on stress relief.

ZESTER/GRATER

A zester or grater is required for some of the recipes containing citrus fruit. Zesting fruit peels is a great way to incorporate concentrated fruit flavor in a cookie. A fine-tooth grater will get the job done, but I've found that the gadgets made specifically for zesting work amazingly smoothly.

OVENS

If you are reading these pages, I will assume that you have an oven that you will soon be using. There are a few things to know about your oven before you begin. Keep the following things in mind when baking the cookies in this book:

1   Preheat your oven to the required temperature and wait at least 5 additional minutes before putting your cookies into the oven. Pretend it's an oversight, so as to prevent trust issues.

2   Shut the oven door quickly after adding the cookies and do not reopen it until the timer beeps (use your light for peeking!).

3   Set the timer for the minimum recommended time listed in the recipe and check every minute after for signs of doneness (lightly browned around bottom edge and no glaring gobs of uncooked dough in the centers).

4   All ovens are different. What works perfectly for my oven might not work for yours.

Higher altitudes (above 3,000 feet) can make baking tricky. However, because of their short bake times, cookies typically do fairly well at higher altitudes compared to other baked goods. Make the following slight adjustments to each recipe if you are above 3,000 feet:

- Decrease leavening agents (baking soda/baking powder) by ⅛ teaspoon (0.6 g) for every teaspoon (4.6 g) used. If less than 1 teaspoon (5 g) is used, don't change a thing.

- Increase the oven temperature slightly (by 15 to 20°F [8.5 to 11.2°C]) and decrease the bake time slightly (by 1 to 2 minutes).

- Increase liquids by 2 tablespoons (30 ml) for every cup (235 ml) used.

- For altitudes over 3,500 feet (0.66 mile), increase the flour by 1 to 2 tbsp (7.5 to 30 g) per recipe.

Ingredients

The first step to ensuring a recipe is going to turn out great is making sure all of the ingredients are fresh! If you use the hard, clumpy brown sugar that has been sitting in your pantry for seven years, your cookies will reflect that. Check package expiration dates and avoid using clumpy, stale, discolored ingredients.

LEAVENING AGENTS (BAKING POWDER AND BAKING SODA)

Making sure your leavening agents are not expired is very important. I always err on the safe side with this because using expired leavening agents can significantly alter baked goods. The moment I pull a container of baking powder or baking soda out of the grocery bag, I write a date exactly six months in the future on the container. When the date arrives, I throw away the container, even if it is half-full, and replace it with another.

Store baking soda and baking powder in a cupboard or pantry that is far from heat or moisture.

EXTRACTS

Some of the recipes in the previous pages require flavor extracts that may not be available at your local grocery store. I had a few of the more unusual extracts shipped to me via Amazon for a couple of dollars each. If you're not up for planning a recipe a few days in advance or springing for an extract that you don't think you will use again, I get it. Recommended substitutions for uncommon extracts are listed within the recipes.

FREEZE-DRIED FRUIT

Freeze-dried fruit is used in a handful of the recipes as a way to add concentrated fruit flavoring to a cookie and I highly recommend not skipping out on this ingredient. *Do not confuse dried or dehydrated fruit with freeze-dried fruit because they are very different products!* During the freeze-drying process, 98 to 99 percent of the moisture in the fruit is removed, making it an ideal option for turning fruit into powder for baking.

FREEZE DRIED VS. DEHYDRATED FRUIT

Freeze-dried fruit can be found near the raisins in most major grocery stores. Trader Joe's and Amazon both carry many types. Walmart sells freeze-dried fruit as well, and offers free in-store pickup for anything found on the Walmart website.

LIQUIDS

When liquids are called for in a recipe, add them to the recipe at room temperature when possible. If it's not possible (and I'll be honest here—I do not always have time for this), cream all the other ingredients together first, then add the cold liquids. Adding cold liquids right away can change the properties of the ingredients, such as making the butter lumpy instead of creamy.

GLUTEN-FREE FLOUR

I did some testing with gluten-free flour blends on a handful of the recipes in this book. I found that Pillsbury Best Multi-purpose Gluten Free Flour Blend was a great replacement for regular all-purpose flour. A blend such as this one that contains xanthan gum will make the batter sticky, the way gluten does in regular flour.

BUTTER

Check the label on your butter before adding it to your mixing bowl. *Margarine and vegetable oil spread are not the same things as butter!* I always use salted butter for baking, but every baker has a different opinion regarding salted vs. unsalted. Basically it comes down to this for me: I love salt, even in my sugary baked goods. If this is too crazy a concept for you, I would suggest first eliminating the salt (if included) from the ingredients list in each recipe. To take it a step further, completely replace salted with unsalted butter and add ¼ teaspoon of salt for every cup (225 g) of butter used in the recipe.

Softening butter before adding it to the mixing bowl is a necessity. Place the required amount of butter into a small, microwave-safe bowl and microwave on high for 30 seconds. The butter should be soft and gooey, but not totally melted. If it appears too solid after 30 seconds, cook it for another 15 seconds. I typically don't ever need to go past the 45-second mark. Alternatively, cut the butter into small chunks and place in a small metal bowl. Submerge the bottom part of the bowl in hot water (not quite boiling) until the butter has softened.

ALCOHOL AND CAFFEINE

There are varying opinions about whether alcohol completely bakes out during the cooking process. A USDA study done in 2003 showed that anywhere from 4 to 85 percent of alcohol remains in a recipe after being cooked, which gives some insight into the debated question. "The assumption that all alcohol is evaporated when heat is applied during cooking is not valid. Cooking always results in some, but not total loss of alcohol. . . . Uncooked and briefly cooked dishes had the highest alcohol retention."[1]

Eight cookies in this book contain alcohol and a handful of those have alcohol within the icing (totally uncooked). I would advise anyone abstaining from alcohol to avoid these recipes completely. When serving or sharing them, have them clearly labeled as containing alcohol. I keep all cookies made with alcohol in a closed container on the top shelf of my fridge with a note. The amount consumed per cookie would likely be minimal but it's better to err on the safe side, especially when children are rifling through the fridge.

Caffeine is an ingredient in a handful of the recipes as well, so treat these cookies the same way you treat the boozy ones. Keep them clearly labeled and do not serve them to adults abstaining from caffeine or to children.

Quick Fixes

Cookie dough can turn out unexpectedly crumbly or gooey even when a recipe is followed exactly and this can typically be fixed quite easily.

If the batter appears super runny beyond what the recipe mentions, add flour 2 tablespoons (15 g) at a time until a firmer consistency has been reached.

If the batter is crumbly and won't stick together, add more of a liquid ingredient from the recipe (such as milk or softened butter) 1 tablespoon (15 ml/g) at a time until a more cohesive consistency is achieved.

Storage

Once a batch of cookies has been made, they should be stored in sealed containers. It will be noted in the instructions when cookies should be refrigerated, although I personally like to refrigerate all of my cookies until I am ready to serve them. This is a personal preference and not necessary for all recipes. I find that this keeps them fresh longer and it also helps the gooier cookies stay firm.

---

1   J. Augustin, E. Augustin, R. L. Curufelli, S. R. Hagen and C. Teitzel, "Alcohol Retention in Food Preparation," *Journal of the American Dietetic Association 92 (1992): 486–88.*

Acknowledgments

There is this strange yet perfect combination of positivity and negativity that drives me to accomplish my goals. I appreciate the people who have looked at me like I was *insaaaaane* when I shared my dreams of becoming a professional blogger and author. Those furrowed brows are scorched into my memory and they have helped me to overcome many feats. More important, though, I remember daily the people who have had faith in me over the years. And there have been many. I have an amazingly supportive bunch of people in my life.

Above all else, Page Street Publishing deserves many thanks for having faith in my ability to create this cookbook. Many thanks to Will and Marissa and the amazing crew at Page Street who have made this project come to life.

My amazing blog readers are really what got me to this point and I am forever grateful for every single eye that has peeked at my beloved website.

I have the best husband a girl could ask for and I am beyond grateful for Dan's support of the work I love so much. He keeps me grounded and breathing and constantly moving forward. Plus he's super cute. My amazing friend Cara was one of the first people to tell me I was going to succeed in my endeavors to become a blogger and author. I am humbled by the faith she had in me, way before I had faith in myself.

My precious boys Elijah and Sammy are my inspiration for everything I do. Heather (a.k.a. Best Friend a Girl Could Ask For) has counseled me through half of my life, including the journey of writing this book, and I love her more than a million batches of Dark Roast Coffee Cookies. Traci (a.k.a. Girl with the Best Ideas) helped me style a handful of the photos in this book. Jane (a.k.a. World's Most Talented Baker) gave me a few brilliant baking tips that I used in this book. Kathy (a.k.a. Kindest Human on the Planet) provided me with a comfortable, quiet space at her home in Reno during the last days of writing this book. Jai (a.k.a. Favorite Hair Expert) helped brainstorm cookie ideas, a few which I used in this book. Many friends and family members gave me constructive feedback that helped make the recipes in this book the best they could possibly be. And I can't possibly go without thanking Kendis and Heather for driving me to urgent care after getting my left ring finger caught in a hand mixer while making a batch of Margarita Cookies. Thankfully there was leftover tequila, not a drop of which went to waste.

About the Author

Megan Porta is a food blogger and author who lives with her husband (who is so handsome that he gets whistled at from car windows), two spunky boys and sweet yellow lab Buddy in Minneapolis. She started her blog in 2010 as a means to leave her graphic design career and spend more time at home with her boys, one of whom has special medical needs. When her employment ended abruptly in 2011, she panicked and then decided it was time to pave her own creative path. Since then she has run a portrait photography business, operated her food blog pipandebby.com and authored her first cookbook, *Cookie Remix*. Her next food-related dreams include (but aren't limited to): running a food truck, being on a cooking show, writing more cookbooks and doing much more blogging. Her work has been published in *Woman's World* and *Southern Living* magazine and she has had repeated online exposure on Huffington Post and BuzzFeed.

Index